Studying for your
Education
Degree

**CRITICAL
STUDY SKILLS**

Critical Study Skills for Education Students

Our new series of study skills texts for education students has four key titles to help you succeed at your degree:

Studying for your Education Degree

Academic Writing and Referencing for your Education Degree

Critical Thinking Skills for your Education Degree

Communication Skills for your Education Degree

Register with **Critical Publishing** to:

- be the first to know about forthcoming education titles;
- find out more about our new series;
- sign up for our regular newsletter for special offers, discount codes and more.

Visit our website at: **www.criticalpublishing.com**

Our titles are also available in a range of electronic formats. To order please go to our website www.criticalpublishing.com or contact our distributor NBN International by telephoning **01752 202301** or emailing orders@nbninternational.com.

Studying for your

Education

Degree

CRITICAL
STUDY SKILLS

JANE BOTTOMLEY, STEVEN PRYJMACHUK AND DAVID WAUGH

First published in 2018 by Critical Publishing Ltd

British Library Cataloguing in Publication Data
A CIP record for this book is available from the British Library

ISBN: 978-1-912096-82-4

This book is also available in the following e-book formats:

MOBI: 978-1-912096-81-7
EPUB: 978-1-912096-80-0
Adobe e-book reader: 978-1-912096-79-4

Text and cover design by Out of House Limited
Project management by Out of House Publishing
Printed in the UK by 4edge, Essex

Critical Publishing
3 Connaught Road
St Albans
AL3 5RX
www.criticalpublishing.com

Paper from responsible sources

Contents

Acknowledgements

We would like to thank the many university and education students who have inspired us to write these books. Thanks are also due to Anita Gill and John Morley.

Jane Bottomley, Steven Pryjmachuk and David Waugh

Meet the series editor and authors

Jane Bottomley

is the **Series Editor** for *Critical Study Skills* and a co-author of all books in the series. She is a Senior Language Tutor at the University of Manchester and a Senior Fellow of the British Association of Lecturers in English for Academic Purposes (BALEAP). She has helped students from a wide range of disciplines to improve their academic skills and achieve their study goals. She has previously published on scientific writing.

Steven Pryjmachuk

is Professor of Mental Health Nursing Education in the School of Health Science's Division of Nursing, Midwifery and Social Work at the University of Manchester and a Senior Fellow of the Higher Education Academy. His teaching, clinical and research work has centred largely on supporting and facilitating individuals – be they students, patients or colleagues – to develop, learn or care independently.

David Waugh

David is Associate Professor of Education at Durham University where he is subject leader for Primary English. He has written more than 40 books on education and has taught in four schools, as well as teaching undergraduates and postgraduates. He has worked in education in universities for 28 years and also regularly teaches in schools, using the four children's novels he has written as a stimulus for reading, writing and discussion.

Introduction

Studying for your Education Degree is the first book in the *Critical Study Skills for Education Students* series. The *Critical Study Skills for Education Students* series supports all students embarking on university-based education undergraduate degrees, including initial teacher training. It is aimed at all such students, including those who have come to university straight from A levels, and those who have travelled a different route, perhaps returning to education after working or raising a family. The books will be of use both to students from the UK, and international students who are preparing to study in a new culture – and perhaps in a second language. The books also include guidance for students with specific learning difficulties.

Studying for your Education Degree introduces you to university life and helps you to understand what you need to know and do to meet the requirements of your degree programme. It guides you through the systems and procedures which you will encounter, at the same time 'demystifying' some aspects of academic culture. It will help you acquire, develop and put into practice the knowledge, skills and strategies you need to succeed at university and in your professional practice. Throughout the book, there is an emphasis on particular aspects of learning which are highly valued in academic life and in the education professions: **learner autonomy**, **critical thinking** and **reflective practice**.

Between them, the authors have many years' experience of education, and academic study skills. All the information, text extracts and activities in the book have a clear education focus and are often directly linked to the **Teachers' Standards**. There is also reference to relevant institutional bodies, books and journals throughout.

The many activities in the book include **reflections**, **case studies**, **top tips** and **tasks**. There are also **advanced skills** sections, which highlight particular knowledge and skills that you will need towards the end of your degree programme – or perhaps if you go on to postgraduate study. The activities often require you to work things out and discover things for yourself, a learning technique which is commonly used in universities. For many activities, there is no right or wrong answer – they might simply require you to reflect on your experience or situations you are likely to encounter at university; for tasks which require a particular response, there is an answer key at the back of the book.

These special features throughout the book are clearly signalled by icons to help you recognise them:

 Learning outcomes;

 Quick quiz or example exam questions/assessment tasks;

 Reflection (a reflective task or activity);

 Task (usually a more practical or written task);

 Case studies;

Top tips;

 Checklist;

 Advanced skills information;

 Answer provided at the back of the book.

Students with limited experience of academic life in the UK will find it helpful to work through the book systematically; more experienced students may wish to 'dip in and out' of the book. Whichever approach you adopt, handy **cross references** signalled in the margins will help you quickly find the information that you need to focus on or revisit.

We hope that this book will help you to develop as an aware, independent, critical and reflective learner and practitioner, and that it will guide you towards success in your chosen study path at university.

In the context of this book, the term 'education' should be taken to include 'educational studies and teacher education', wherever this is not explicitly stated. There is an **Appendix** on the **language of higher education** at the back of the book which you can consult as you work through the text.

Chapter 1
Studying education in higher education

Learning outcomes

After reading this chapter you will:

- have gained knowledge of higher education and its place in the UK education system;

- understand some of the terminology and 'jargon' used in higher education;

- have gained knowledge of institutions which set standards for education training;

- have gained knowledge of levels and qualifications in education;

- understand the relevance and importance of lifelong learning and continuing professional development;

- understand the importance of student autonomy and independent learning in universities;

- have gained knowledge of how courses are structured and delivered.

This chapter will develop your knowledge and understanding of the study of education in UK universities. It will outline the 'qualification frameworks' that are relevant to becoming, and developing as, an educator, and discuss the role of important educational and professional bodies. In addition, you will be introduced to the types of teaching and learning that you will encounter as a student teacher.

Before you read the chapter, test your knowledge with the **Quick quiz** below. You can revisit the quiz as you read, or come back to it after reading the whole chapter to see if your answers have changed. Key words in this chapter are highlighted in **bold** and can be found in the Appendix.

CROSS
REFERENCE

Appendix,
The language
of higher
education

Quick quiz

1) What does HE stand for?

2) How is HE different from FE?

3) What are the main qualifications offered by universities?

4) Which is the higher level qualification, a *degree* or a *diploma*?

5) What is the minimum academic qualification you need to become a qualified teacher?

6) What mark (percentage) do you usually need to obtain a *first-class* degree?

7) What are 'credits' and how can you get them?

8) What is 'lifelong learning'?

9) What are the most common types of assessment in universities?

What is HE?

HE stands for '**higher education**', one of two options in UK **tertiary education**, ie education available to people of 16 years or above.

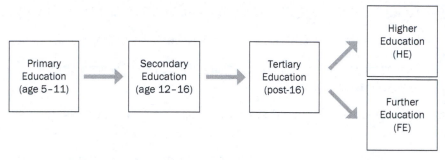

Figure 1.1: The UK education system

HE is mainly provided by universities, and principally awards **degrees** and **diplomas**. In contrast, **further education (FE)** is provided by colleges, which deliver courses and award qualifications which are **vocational** in nature (NVQs; City & Guilds; BTEC), preparing people directly for the workplace. However, in recent years, there has been a blurring of the line between the two types of institution, with many FE colleges, sometimes in association with partner universities, also offering degrees. This is one way of making degrees accessible to a wider range of people, some of whom may find it convenient to attend classes in a local FE college or to study in the evenings. Recently introduced 'degree apprenticeships', which offer the potential to obtain a degree while learning on the job, also blur the boundaries between vocational and academic learning.

Your education degree

Teacher training, which forms part of most education degrees in the UK, is today fully integrated into the HE sector. There are some routes into teaching in which the universities' involvement is more limited, but these tend to be at postgraduate level and require trainees to possess a degree qualification. Although there is a large vocational component to teaching, based on practical teaching skills, teaching also requires highly developed intellectual skills, and universities are considered to be the best place for undergraduate students to acquire and develop these. Education is thus an academic subject, equivalent to any other, such as medicine, engineering or English literature, and therefore measured against the same standards.

Qualification frameworks

HE qualifications, sometimes called 'academic awards', are regulated across the UK via two frameworks: the Quality Assurance Agency for Higher Education in England, Wales and Northern Ireland (QAA, 2008), and the Quality Assurance Agency for Higher Education in Scotland (QAA, 2014). These frameworks help institutions and employers judge the value of an individual's education and help ensure equity between academic subjects. Table 1.1 shows the academic levels

Table 1.1: An overview of academic levels in relation to education study in HE

UNDERGRADUATE STUDY			
England, Wales, Northern Ireland	**Scotland**	**Award**	**Notes**
Level 4	Level 7	Certificate of Higher Education (CertHE)	
Level 5	Level 8	Diploma of Higher Education (DipHE) Foundation Degree (FdD)	
Level 6	Level 9	Ordinary Bachelor's Degree eg BA Education	
	Level 10	Bachelor's Degree with Honours eg BA Education, BA (Hons) Education with QTS	BA Education with QTS is the usual qualification at undergraduate level to teach.
POSTGRADUATE STUDY			
Level 7	Level 11	Master's Degree eg MSc, MA, MPhil Postgraduate Certificate of Education (PGCE)	PGCE is the HE qualification at postgraduate level to teach.
Level 8	Level 12	Research Doctorate (PhD) Professional Doctorate eg DPhil Education, PhD Education, EdD	Sometimes undertaken by practising teachers and often taken by teacher trainers in HE

assigned by the QAA to each stage of HE, and provides information on how they relate to a study pathway in education.

An undergraduate degree has four classifications. These are shown in Table 1.2, along with the marks usually required at each level.

CROSS REFERENCE

Chapter 6, Assessment

Table 1.2: Bachelor's degree classifications and typical required marks

CLASSIFICATION	MARKS REQUIRED
1st	Above 70%
2:1	60–69%
2:2	50–59%
3rd	40–49%
Fail	Below 40%

Courses and credits

You can see from Table 1.1 that, in order to enter the teaching profession, you must obtain a degree from an HE institution, usually a university. If you study full time, it will take three years to obtain an honours degree (or four years in Scotland). However, universities recognise that timescale is not possible or ideal for many people, so they have flexible learning systems which allow students to fit study into their lives in a practical way. This can involve:

- **distance learning**, where the student mainly studies from home via correspondence, using web-based resources – perhaps occasionally attending university workshops etc;
- **blended learning**, which combines traditional classroom study and web-based learning;
- **part-time study** (including the new degree apprenticeships mentioned earlier).

Flexible learning is facilitated by the **credit** points system which underpins HE education. Each course **module** that you study has a number of credit points attached to it. Each credit is equal to 10 hours of study, either in class, or through self-study (QAA, 2008, 2014). These credit points build up to eventually form your degree, whether over three years' full-time study, or over a longer period if you study part time. Table 1.3 shows that a student has to earn 360 credit points in order to be awarded an honours degree.

Table 1.3: HE qualifications in relation to credit points

ACADEMIC QUALIFICATION	CREDIT POINTS REQUIRED
CertHE	120 at Level 4 (Scotland Level 7)
DipHE	120 at Level 4 (Scotland Level 7) + 120 at Level 5 (Scotland Level 8)

ACADEMIC QUALIFICATION	CREDIT POINTS REQUIRED
Degree with Honours (Ordinary Degree in Scotland)	120 at Level 4 (Scotland Level 7) + 120 at Level 5 (Scotland Level 8) + 120 at Level 6 (Scotland Level 9)

Look at the QAA frameworks (2008, 2014) online to see descriptors detailing exactly what is expected of a student at each level. Note that not all universities offer the CertHE. Some universities in England, Wales and Northern Ireland may offer an ordinary degree without honours to students who have obtained a certain number of credits at Level 6. A four-year Scottish Honours Degree requires an additional 120 credits at Level 9/10.

Universities provide students with information on each module with regard to its academic level and the number of credit points it carries. Many modules, often called 'core modules', will be obligatory; some modules will be optional. All modules are organised around the following:

- a set of **learning outcomes** which identify what you will be able to do or understand by the end of the course;
- a process of **teaching and learning** which will help you achieve the learning outcomes;
- **assessment** which will measure your achievement and provide evidence of it.

Top tips

Thinking about 'the big picture'

Learning outcomes, teaching and learning, and assessment will be aligned, so you should think about 'the big picture' and consider them together. When preparing for assessments, for example, look again at the learning outcomes to check what you will be expected to demonstrate. In class, think about how the classroom activities are partly preparing you for assessment, and ask if you are not sure.

Lifelong learning and continuous professional development

The flexible approach to study outlined above is underpinned by the much-valued educational principle of **lifelong learning**. Lifelong learning, by definition, extends beyond your degree, and may involve postgraduate study or **continuing professional development (CPD)**. CPD in teaching can be provided by a range of organisations, including local education authorities, private consultancies, multi-academy trusts and higher education institutions. It is important to discuss your CPD needs with your line manager or mentor once you have begun teaching.

Case study

How is CPD demonstrated in the personal account below?

I have been teaching for five years in two primary schools, having moved after my third year to take up a post as literacy co-ordinator. During this time, I have attended a range of courses in order to address aspects of my practice where I felt I could develop my skills and knowledge. After attending a series of twilight workshops at my local university's school of education, I joined the United Kingdom Literacy Association and went to a conference with two colleagues. This stimulated two of us to enrol at the university to take a master's degree and to focus, for our dissertations, on aspects of literacy. My studies have enabled me to look at the way in which spelling is currently taught in schools and to consider strategies for developing spelling in my own school. This was a key focus following the school's last Ofsted inspection, and the school is subsidising my tuition fees as it considers that my research will benefit teaching and learning.

Reflection

What do you think your CPD priorities might be when you are a qualified teacher?

Being a university student

Reflection

What is your previous experience of study? Which of the following have you experienced? Was your experience positive or negative? Why was this?

1) Big classes where the teacher talks a lot and the class mostly listens

2) Large lectures with hundreds of students

3) Small seminar groups where people discuss topics or articles

4) One-to-one tutorials with a teacher

University culture and practices may not always reflect your past educational experiences. Some students may find it difficult to work things out at first.

Case studies

Do you think these students have a good understanding of what is expected of them at university level? What advice would you give them?

1) "My course looks quite easy – there aren't many lectures and I don't have to hand in any essays until the end of the semester. So it looks like I'll have a lot of free time!"

2) "The lecturer puts some things on Blackboard after the lecture, but I'm not very confident with technical stuff so I haven't seen it."

3) "It doesn't matter if I miss lectures – I can get all the information I need from reading textbooks."

4) "I'm very nervous about speaking in front of people so I tend to keep my head down in seminars and just get through them without drawing attention to myself."

5) "I'm disappointed in my essay mark and don't understand what I did wrong – I worked really hard on it! But there's nothing I can do about it now. Maybe I'm just not cut out for this."

The students quoted above have some common misunderstandings about university life. These areas of confusion are dealt with in the following sections, to demonstrate, among other things, how study is not just about the time you spend in the classroom, why it is important to go to lectures, when and how you should seek support from academic staff, and why, sometimes, you might just need to push yourself beyond your comfort zone in order to achieve your full potential!

Study time

At university, you will encounter a range of teaching and learning methods, including those which involve face-to-face contact with academic staff, ie **lectures**, **seminars** and **tutorials**. However, you may find that there seems to be a lot of 'free' time on your timetable. Hence, it is important to understand that the time you spend with your lecturers is only a small part of your study. A 10-credit module is seen to represent approximately 100 hours of actual work (QAA, 2008, 2014). So if you attend, say, 30 hours of lectures on a particular 10-credit module, this still leaves 70 hours of study to complete outside the classroom. This may involve searching the library, reading, planning and writing essays, improving your computer skills, or collaborating with other students on a group project.

CROSS REFERENCE

Chapter 2, Strategies for effective learning

Top tips

Getting the most from your study time

Try thinking of your full-time studies as a typical 'working week' of about 35–40 hours a week, 7–8 hours a day, and plan your time accordingly. (Adapt this if you are studying part time.) Take sensible breaks throughout the day, just as you would if you were working — maybe cook a nice healthy lunch to give you energy, or take the dog for a walk to give your brain some much-needed downtime!

Virtual Learning Environments

Study outside the classroom is often facilitated by Virtual Learning Environments (VLEs) such as **Blackboard** or **Moodle**. VLEs contain vital information on the course and links to useful resources. They also host a number of useful tools. For example, VLE discussion boards can enable interaction with your peers and with the lecturers. VLEs are also important in terms of assessment: you may be required to complete some assessment tasks online, and you will probably be required to upload written assignments onto your VLE using plagiarism-detection software such as **Turnitin**, which compares your writing with published sources and other submitted essays to ensure it is all your own work. You may also receive assessment feedback online through tools such as **Feedback Studio**.

Top tips

Getting the most from your VLE

1) Check your VLE frequently as there may be new announcements or documents. Staff will just assume that you will look at these; they will not chase you up to make sure you've accessed them. It is your responsibility to be on top of things.

2) Spend some time learning how to navigate the site so that you can access things quickly when you need them. The more you use the site, the easier this will get.

3) Read your discussion board contributions carefully before clicking 'send'. Make sure that the style is appropriately polite and that there is no ambiguity – especially if it could cause offence. Also check your grammar and punctuation – poor writing can detract from the seriousness of your message.

4) Check if it's possible to download slides before lectures – this could help you to be more prepared for lectures, and facilitate the note-taking process.

Lectures

Lectures at university are designed to provide an overview of a topic. As such, they are a very useful starting point. They are also a springboard for further reading, thinking, discussion and writing. The aim of lectures is not just to reproduce what is in the books: the lecturer can guide you towards the most important aspects of a topic, or provide you with a theoretical framework on which to 'hang' the ideas you accumulate from your reading. They may direct you towards particular chapters in textbooks or indicate how different journal articles relate to the topic, as well as each other. Lectures can also be enjoyable! A lecturer may present you with interesting examples, or offer up lively anecdotes which can bring a subject to life. Some lecturers may include interactive activities, for example, getting you to use mobile phone apps or 'clickers' (a device used to provide on-the-spot analysis of students' responses during a lecture), or they may encourage comments and questions.

Top tips

Getting the most from lectures

1) Experiment with different note-taking strategies: linear notes, mind maps, diagrams etc.

2) Use headings and sub-headings to organise your notes, or use colour to highlight thematic patterns.

3) Experiment with taking hand-written notes and using your laptop or tablet to see which suits you best.

4) Put together a list of useful abbreviations and get into the habit of using them. Some common ones are listed below. Match them to the full term (as with the example that has been given) to check your understanding:

   eg   that is to say
   NB   compare and contrast
   cf   for example
   ie   note

5) If you find it difficult to keep up in lectures, ask if the lecturer is willing to upload the lecture slides onto the VLE beforehand, so that you can do some preparation and maybe check out some difficult terminology beforehand. If the slides are available, you could upload them onto your laptop or tablet and annotate them as you follow the lecture.

6) Go over your notes as soon as possible after the lecture, when it is fresh in your mind. Improve the organisation if you can, adding or refining headings, sub-headings and cross references – this is easier of course with wordprocessed notes.

7) Find a lecture 'buddy' who you can discuss the lecture with afterwards. You could check if you agree on what the main points are, or try to clarify anything you were confused about.

8) Look back at previous lecture notes before attending the next one.

Seminars

On some courses, small seminar groups will provide an opportunity for you to follow up on the lecture, to clarify points and expand your understanding. You may be asked to read an article beforehand, and one or two students may be asked to lead the seminar by presenting their summary and opinion of the article, before a general group discussion.

It can be difficult to contribute in seminars: for some people it is rather nerve-wracking; many find it hard to interject – particularly if there are some dominant personalities (maybe yours!) in the room. But remember you are all in the same boat – you all have your strengths and weaknesses, you all have something to learn – and the lecturer is there to bring out the best in you, not put you on the spot!

Top tips

Getting the most from seminars

1) Be prepared. Think about two or three points you would like to make, and think about how you might express them.

2) Say something early on in the seminar if you can. Once you take the plunge and contribute, the second time will be much easier.

3) Use seminars as an opportunity to 'talk through' and test ideas that you are exploring. This can often be a good way of preparing for an essay.

4) Don't be afraid to ask for clarification – if you haven't understood something, then there is a good chance that others haven't either!

5) Be prepared to provide clarification yourself. It is often necessary to reconsider the way we express ourselves in order to achieve clarity; this reformulation process is also a way of helping us to understand if we have truly grasped an idea.

6) Listening is just as important as speaking. Be prepared to learn from others – and to challenge them (politely) when you disagree.

7) There is a certain etiquette to be followed in seminars. It is expected that people will disagree with each other on some points, but this is usually done in a very careful way, often using 'balanced' expressions such as:

"I see what you mean, but …"

"I take your point, but …"

"I agree to some extent, but …"

Some 'negative' questions (considered less direct than normal questions) are also useful, eg:

"Wouldn't you say that …?"

"Don't you think that …?"

"Isn't it the case that …?"

"Aren't we forgetting the impact of …?"

CROSS
REFERENCE

Communi-
cation Skills,
Chapter 2,
Participating
in seminars
and meetings

Tutorials

Some universities and courses will offer one-to-one tutorials with a lecturer, often to discuss general progress, give feedback, or help you prepare for an essay or dissertation. Most academic staff will also have **office hours**, when you can visit them in their office and raise any queries. If you are worried about your progress or your marks, it is important that you use this opportunity to seek advice.

Top tips

Getting the most from tutorials

1) Be prepared. The lecturer's time is probably very limited, so spend some time thinking about how you can make the best use of a meeting by preparing some focused questions.

2) Questions which are 'closed', ie questions which simply require a *yes/no* answer, are quicker and easier to deal with than questions which are 'open'. Compare:

   "How should I obtain my data?" (open question)

   "Would a questionnaire be a good way of collecting data in this case?" (closed question)

   The first question puts the onus on the lecturer and requires them to do all the thinking. The second question shows you have thought about things and are now merely making good use of the expertise of the lecturer. The second question is not only easier and quicker to deal with, it also shows that you are taking responsibility for your learning, which will probably lead to a better relationship with the lecturer.

3) If you are not sure you've understood something, briefly summarise the message you think you are receiving from the lecturer to double check.

Independent learning

Studying as an adult at university may be very different to what you experienced at school. At school, for many reasons, there may have been a lot of direct instruction from the teachers, where they talk and you listen. At university, there is more emphasis on guiding you towards working and thinking independently, with the lecturer acting as a facilitator, adviser or resource: this is known as **independent learning**, something which is highly valued in universities.

As a university student, you are expected to take responsibility for, and manage, your own learning at all times. This involves recognising what you need to do to study successfully, and finding out how to do it. Independent learning requires self-motivation, self-direction and self-discipline. The lecturers will guide you; they will offer support and encouragement. But they will not hold your hand; they will not do your work for you or solve your problems. This is not because they are lazy or don't care what their students do; it is because they believe in the educational principle of **student autonomy**, whereby a student takes charge of their own learning. They are convinced that encouraging you to take responsibility for your learning will make you a better student, a better thinker and, ultimately, a better teacher: it will, among other things, prepare you for the requirement to 'take responsibility for improving teaching through appropriate professional development, responding to advice and feedback from colleagues' (TS 8; DfE 2013).

CROSS REFERENCE

Chapter 2, Strategies for effective learning, Managing your learning: student autonomy

CROSS REFERENCE

Communication Skills, Chapter 3, Getting the most from tutorials

CROSS REFERENCE

Chapter 2, Strategies for effective learning, Collaborative learning

A commitment to independent learning is part of a kind of contract between you and the university. This contract also covers the things you can in turn expect from the university.

Top tips

Knowing your rights and responsibilities

Make sure you look at your university's 'Student Charter', sometimes called an 'Educational Contract', a document which tells you what you should expect from the university, and details your own responsibilities as a student.

CROSS
REFERENCE

Chapter 2,
Strategies
for effective
learning,
Managing
your learning:
student
autonomy

One teaching and learning method commonly adopted by university lecturers to encourage independent learning is **directed study**. This is where the lecturer sets a task and offers some guidance; but it is your responsibility to complete the task, even if you are not required to formally submit it. Some tasks are assessed, but others may simply have the aim of contributing to your long-term development. Directed study may involve **problem-based learning**, where you find solutions to real-world problems. This is often achieved by means of **collaborative learning**, ie working collectively and co-operatively with other students. The lecturer may or may not be present; they may or may not intervene. You, the students, are in control of the learning process. During these tasks, you will develop skills which are essential for teaching, in which you are required to develop effective professional relationships with colleagues, knowing how and when to draw on advice and specialist support (TS 8; DfE 2013).

CROSS
REFERENCE

Chapter 4,
Critical
thinking

One of the main aims of activities such as problem-based learning is to help you develop your **critical thinking** skills, your ability to analyse and evaluate information and ideas. Great emphasis is placed on critical thinking in education and in teaching.

In the university learning environment, there may be a certain amount of role reversal in class, whereby a student takes on a typical teacher role. This could include giving a presentation or leading a seminar. Many students can feel very nervous about this kind of activity, but remember there are techniques you can adopt to help you perform better.

For information on how you are assessed at university, see Chapter 6.

Summary

This chapter has examined the place of education and teaching in the UK HE system, and the role of key institutions that set standards for teaching, such as the QAA and the DfE. It has discussed the practicalities of education study in terms of the qualifications and degree classes that can be awarded, as well as the credits system that underpins university courses. It has explored the notion of lifelong learning, and it has looked closely at current modes of teaching and learning, with a particular emphasis on independent learning and student autonomy. With this knowledge and understanding, you will be well-equipped to begin your journey as a trainee teacher.

CROSS REFERENCE

Chapter 6, Assessment

References

DfE (2013) *Teachers' Standards: Guidance for School Leaders, School Staff and Governing Bodies.* London: DfE.

QAA (Quality Assurance Agency for Higher Education) (2008) *The Framework for Higher Education Qualifications in England, Wales and Northern Ireland* [online]. Available at: www.qaa.ac.uk/en/Publications/Documents/Framework-Higher-Education-Qualifications-08.pdf (accessed 16 February 2018).

QAA (2014) *The Framework for Higher Education Institutions in Scotland* [online]. Available at: www.qaa.ac.uk/en/Publications/Documents/FQHEIS-June-2014.pdf (accessed 16 February 2018).

Chapter 2
Strategies for effective learning

Learning outcomes

After reading this chapter you will:

- have improved your understanding of the learning process;

- have developed strategies for managing your university studies effectively;

- have learned about different theories of learning and understand what kind of learning styles can be effective for you;

- be able to adapt to situations that require you to work independently or collaboratively.

This chapter will explore ideas around learning and enable you to identify which learning strategies could help you meet the expectations of university study. Adopting the right approach to your studies will maximise your potential and enable you to reach your goals.

What is learning?

When you learn, it may be for 'learning's sake', ie to satisfy your curiosity, to improve your mind and to grow as an individual. Or you may learn for a defined purpose or goal. Being a university student ideally involves both these aspects of learning.

Learning is not a question of pouring information and ideas into an empty student vessel! Nor is it something which will just happen as a matter of course if you simply turn up to class. Some learning may be more or less 'unconscious', ie when you just 'pick things up' without really realising it at the time. But most learning, particularly in an academic context, is an active process which requires specific intellectual skills.

Learning is not just a question of finding and remembering facts. It involves many stages and processes as you encounter and explore new information and ideas. Figure 2.1 gives some examples (adapted from Devine, 1987: xix).

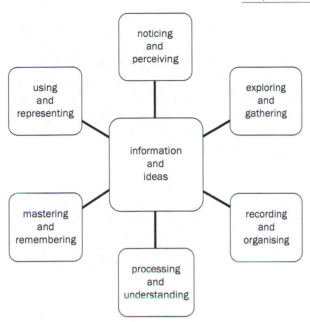

Figure 2.1: The learning process

Something like 'noticing' may seem like a very basic human activity, but noticing key facts, patterns and relationships is actually an essential part of being an intelligent, critical learner, and, importantly, it is something that you can get better at. As you explore, gather, record, and organise facts and ideas, you are employing your analytical and evaluative skills to reveal and understand how things relate and compare. This is how you begin to process and assimilate information and ideas. This processing continues as you work to make sense of all you have learned. When you use and represent the knowledge and understanding you have acquired, in an essay for example, you demonstrate your understanding of the subject, proving that learning has actually occurred!

As you study at university, there are three questions you need to ask:

- *What* do I need to learn?
- *Why* do I need to learn it?
- *How* should I learn it?

This chapter will help you work out *how* you can learn most effectively. If you can find ways of learning which suit your personality and circumstances, draw on the qualities and skills you already possess to some degree, and encourage personal and intellectual development, you are much more likely to enjoy and benefit from the learning process.

Managing your learning: student autonomy

Universities have identified a set of 'graduate attributes' that students should develop as they pursue their studies (discussed in more detail in Chapter 3).

CROSS REFERENCE

Chapter 3, Becoming a member of your academic and professional community, Graduate attributes

CROSS
REFERENCE

Chapter 3,
Becoming
a member
of your
academic and
professional
community,
Reflective
practice

One key graduate attribute is *personal and intellectual autonomy* (Jenkins, 2009). Being autonomous means managing your own learning, and taking responsibility for it. This means you should be able to recognise and address your own learning needs, and to work out – through experimentation – which learning styles or strategies will serve you best. You need to develop an awareness of which qualities and skills facilitate learning, and consider how you can personally improve in these areas. All of this is underpinned by one particular quality: the capacity for **reflection**, ie standing back from a situation or experience in order to critically analyse and evaluate it so that you can understand and learn from it. This is something which is also central in a teacher's reflective practice. Indeed, the Teachers' Standards require teachers to 'reflect systematically on the effectiveness of lessons and approaches to teaching' (TS 4; DfE 2013).

Autonomy is not always easy to achieve, but it should ultimately make you more effective in your studies and in your professional life. It could also make you happier! Surveys often reveal a strong correlation between autonomy and job satisfaction (see for example, Marks, 2014).

The qualities and skills which can facilitate autonomous learning, such as being reflective, organised or proactive, you no doubt already demonstrate to a greater or lesser extent in your everyday life. University is a chance to develop them still further, with a view to applying them across your studies and in your future professional life. This is why universities use the terms 'graduate attributes' or 'transferable skills', which explicitly link your development at university with your overall personal development and future endeavours.

Reflection

1) Consider some of the main qualities and skills associated with student autonomy and successful learning:

good organisation, discipline, being realistic, resilience, being positive, being pro-active, commitment, motivation, being determined, flexibility, adaptability, innovation, initiative, being open-minded, intellectual curiosity, creativity, reflection, self-awareness

2) Think of situations where you have demonstrated some of these in your everyday life, and areas of your current studies where you might apply them successfully. (Some examples have been given.)

QUALITY/ATTITUDE	EVERYDAY LIFE	CURRENT STUDIES
Being well organised	eg managing my children's after-school activities	eg could organise my lecture notes better using file dividers
Being disciplined	eg writing a shopping list before going to the supermarket – and sticking to it!	eg should put my phone on silent and out of reach while studying
Being resilient (eg recovering from setbacks, persevering, keeping a sense of perspective)	eg took my driving test three times and eventually passed	eg should try to talk to lecturers about negative feedback on an essay to see how I can improve next time – instead of burying my head in the sand!

Strategies for effective learning

You will have opportunities to develop the qualities and skills in the reflection above throughout your studies at university. This section provides you with some general advice to get you started in the right direction.

Being organised

1) Use simple organisational tools to plan your time, activities and environment. These could include:

   - weekly timetables – universities often put individual weekly timetables online via the student portal;
   - academic diaries (from September to June), to record classes, events, exams, deadlines etc;
   - electronic calendars like Microsoft Outlook – your university will probably provide training for these;
   - notebooks or smart phones – jot down or store to-do items as they come to you and transfer them to a more permanent format later if necessary.

2) Include independent study periods on your timetable, with details on what, where and how you plan to study.

3) Remember to factor in the rest of your life! Many students have to juggle study with work, bringing up a family, or an important interest, hobby or commitment. Include these things in your calendars, timetables or diaries.

4) Organise your work space at home. Make it clear to others that this is where you work and that it is important to you.

5) Plan ahead. Plan to get your assignment finished well before the deadline. This will leave you enough time to read through and make minor alterations or corrections. It also means that you will not get stressed by last-minute issues with computers or printers.

Being disciplined

1) Prioritise the tasks on your to-do list, allot a reasonable amount of time to each one, and stick to this.

2) Identify times when you could feasibly study, and make sure that study time is really study time. Use any formally scheduled independent study or reading time to do just that – study and read!

3) Don't allow study to spill over too much into non-study time. Maintain clear boundaries, otherwise you may become over-tired and demotivated.

4) Make a start. Beware of 'displacement activities', chores around the home that suddenly seem more urgent when you are due to start that essay! Make yourself do at least 30 minutes study before doing anything else. By that time, you may have found a 'way into' your essay and the work may seem less daunting; if you are still 'stuck', then leaving it alone for a while and occupying yourself with something else (like the ironing!) may be the sensible option.

5) Take regular breaks. Your brain will get tired, and work may well look different when you look at it with fresh eyes.

Being realistic

1) Do not use studying as an excuse to banish friends, exercise, reading or housework from your life. It is not practical or effective to spend all your time studying, and you will probably lose concentration and get distracted anyway. Also, if you lose control of important aspects of your life, such as keeping on top of your finances, you will only end up worrying when you should be studying or sleeping. It is important to achieve a work–life balance.

2) Remember that your studies also include teaching practice, and it is likely that your academic year will be longer and more demanding than that of students studying other disciplines. This means that, while it is important that you experience normal student life, you may have to moderate your activities. For example, it is clearly not a good idea to go to a student party the night before you are working in a school.

Being smart

1) Multitask by, for example, reading or listening to an educational podcast on the bus.

2) Develop efficient note-taking strategies when reading or in lectures. Think about using a laptop or tablet.

3) If you have module options, make sure you choose the right ones. It is important to choose things that you are most interested in, if you can, but it is also important to consider which options will help you achieve your short- and long-term goals. For example, you may choose an option related to where you want to work when qualified.

4) Learn what is valued in your discipline, and what will get you good marks. For example, as mentioned earlier in this chapter, **reflective practice** is critical to

teaching and it is unlikely that you will get good marks in the later years of your programme if you haven't grasped this concept.

5) Always seek out and follow guidelines and protocols for teaching. And while you are expected to think critically and challenge guidelines and protocols where there is a lack of evidence to support them, make sure you do this tactfully, by discussing things calmly with your mentor, for example; otherwise you could be seen as ill-informed and biased.

6) Make yourself aware of individual staff preferences. There may be general departmental guidelines on formatting, for instance, but you may find that some lecturers prefer you to use 1.5 spacing, whereas others prefer double spacing. (Others may not have a preference, as long as you are clear and consistent.) Remember that you want to make the *actual* reader's experience as smooth and enjoyable as possible, so it is worth spending time considering how you can do this.

Being positive

1) Embrace positive thinking. Being a student is going to be a big part of your life for a long time, so it is important that studying doesn't become some terrible chore that you constantly dread. You will be a better student if you can find as much of the learning process as possible interesting and enjoyable. Some of it may even be fun!

2) You will make many lifelong friends on your course, friends you will be able to turn to and share with when things get tough. They will no doubt have had similar experiences.

Being proactive

1) If you don't know something, think about how you can find it out; if you don't know how to do something, think about how you might work it out. You will find a lot of helpful information in course handbooks and on VLEs. You will be expected to read the relevant documentation regarding the aims, learning outcomes, content and assessments relating to each of your courses, and to seek guidance if there is something that you don't understand.

2) See the big picture. Try not to look at tasks in isolation: find out how they fit into the course overall. Consider not only why you are being asked to do something, but why you are being asked to do something at a particular time or in a particular way. For example, a course on 'research methods' may seem quite abstract to you at the beginning of your studies, but if you look at the information provided in the course handbook on the research dissertation you may be required to carry out in the future, it will make more sense to you.

3) Some people find it easier to manage their studies if they arrange to work with others. If you are alone, it can be very easy to find those 'displacement activities': that pile of ironing can suddenly seem quite tempting compared to a pile of heavy reading! But if you've committed to a study meeting with others, you probably won't want to let them down. Just remember that studying together must not lead to collusion: you can learn together, but, unless it is a group assignment, that

learning must then be directed into an individual assessment which is entirely your own work.

4) If you have, or think you may have, a specific learning difficulty, seek support. Universities have special departments which are likely to be able to provide services to meet your needs.

5) Note that being 'supernumerary' in teaching practice, ie additional to the school's teaching staff, does not mean you cannot or should not take part in teaching activities. Use every opportunity to learn and demonstrate your abilities, whatever stage you are at in your teaching course. Don't wait to be asked to work with pupils: ask colleagues how you can help.

Being committed

1) Commit yourself to your studies. It can be tempting to believe that getting things out of the way with as little effort as possible will bring satisfaction, but often, students report that the most satisfying tasks are those they put the most effort into. Looking at an essay that you've rushed off at the last minute can be a very dispiriting experience. It's something you've probably detached from because you just want it out of the way. On the other hand, printing out an essay that has been carefully considered and crafted, up to and including precise formatting, will usually bring you a great deal of satisfaction. And, whatever mark you receive, if it's for an essay you care about, it will mean more to you. If it's a good mark, you will feel proud and motivated to continue in the same vein; if it's a disappointing mark, you will care more about obtaining feedback, and the criticisms will probably relate more to concrete things you can change. If you receive a poor mark for a slap-dash essay, you already know why you've done badly!

2) Commitment means doing everything you can to manage your own circumstances at any given time. This includes contacting your tutors and lecturers when you have academic and/or personal issues, rather than burying your head in the sand or plodding on heroically. They are very experienced in student matters and you probably won't be telling them anything they haven't heard before.

Being open-minded

1) Be aware of the benefits that could come through working with others. Be alert to what you can learn from those around you, including other students.

2) Education is constantly changing, so you need to get used to change. Try to approach change as an opportunity rather than an irritation – unless you have real professional concerns about it, in which case raise them with a mentor or tutor.

3) Accept that you will, like everyone, experience uncertainty at times, and that it is no shame to admit this: it is all part of the learning process.

Being reflective and self-aware

1) Everyone makes mistakes. The important thing is to learn from them. It is also important to be conscious of and confident about what you do well. After all, if

you are not aware of your own strengths and limitations, how will you be able to help colleagues and students work on theirs?

2) Think about how you can use feedback from lecturers and your peers to improve your performance.

3) Learn to look at your own work with a critical eye. Try reading an essay out loud to see if it makes sense, for example.

4) Compile a reflective journal to record your responses to your student and teaching experiences.

5) Understand your own learning preferences, and the alternatives available to you, and be prepared to experiment. This will be discussed in the next section.

Learning styles

A learning style is a particular way of acquiring, processing and using information or ideas. At this stage in your life, you will have developed certain approaches to learning new things. The premise in this chapter is that there is no right or wrong way to study, but that it is beneficial for students to explore options and to experiment. In this section, you are encouraged to reflect on your experience and to consider some theories of learning. This process may confirm your intuitions about what is best for you, or it might persuade you to investigate alternative approaches to learning.

Reflection

1) Think of things you have learned to do in the past (eg learning to drive or swim, learning a language or a new technology, learning karate or Zumba).

2) Which were positive learning experiences?

3) Which were negative learning experiences?

4) What is it that made them successful or not?

5) Which of these things were within or outside of your control?

While reflecting on your past learning experiences, you may have identified certain common threads in your approach to learning, and these may be reflected in the many theories of learning which exist. These theories are of interest to students because they can suggest useful learning strategies. However, there is disagreement about their validity, and so they should be viewed with a critical eye.

Some theories of learning suggest that your learning behaviour and preferences are connected to your personality. One of the most well known (though not universally accepted – see Willingham et al, 2015) of these suggests that different people learn better through different senses.

- **Visual** learners are said to learn better when they can see things. This may involve reading or watching videos. They are advised to use colour coding and pictures in their notes.

- **Aural/Auditory** learners are said to learn better when they can hear things and speak to people. This may involve reading the essays they've written out loud. They are advised to meet regularly with other students to talk through prescribed reading or assessment tasks, and to use podcasts.
- **Kinaesthetic** learners are said to learn better when they can touch things or bring out the physical side of something. This may involve creating posters or investigating issues through role play. They are advised to organise information onto interactive physical charts or picture boards.

This sensory model is sometimes referred to as the VAK model (Dunn et al, 1984), later expanded to the VARK model, which includes **Reading and Writing** preferences (Fleming and Mills, 1992). Alternative theories of learning divide people along other lines, according to whether they are, for example, introvert or extrovert, visual or verbal, intuitive or analytical. Honey and Mumford (1982) divide people into four learning types: activists, reflectors, theorists or pragmatists. They suggest that most people are likely to stick to one or two of these, depending on their personality. However, they also propose that some of these styles are better suited to particular types of *activity*, concluding, therefore, that it is important for everyone to develop a range of approaches.

Being aware of these different learning models and the ideas behind them offers you an opportunity to think how you might personalise your learning. However, as mentioned above, some scholars question the evidence base of these theories of learning (see for example, Willingham et al, 2015), so it is important to assess them critically. Keep an open mind, but do not label yourself or restrict the options available to you. And remember the importance of the learning context, the conditions under which you learn, or the nature of the task or activity with which you are faced. What's more, be aware that things don't always go to plan, as demonstrated in the case studies below.

Case studies

Consider the following situations. What advice would you give?

1) Lectures send Sarah to sleep! The problem, however, is that lectures are an important part of the course and attendance is monitored. What is the solution?

2) Craig feels more engaged with his studies when he works with others. He meets a great group of like-minded people on his course. He invites them round to his halls, and together they produce an impressive piece of work for the next assignment. What problems might Craig and his friends encounter?

3) Wen Li is a night owl! She works best at night: this is when her mind really gets going, and she can often work productively until the early hours of the morning. However, she is scheduled to do a week of early starts (7.30 am) in a school. How will she be able to maintain her previously successful strategy?

4) Eva is a single parent. She has family help with childcare in the day time but in the evening, with the TV on all the time, and phones constantly on the go, she finds it hard to find the quiet space with no distractions that suits her. What can she do?

Discussion of case studies

There are no simple answers to the problems described in the case studies above, but it is worth considering the following if you find yourself in a similar situation:

1) Sometimes it is necessary to do things you don't enjoy. Question whether there is something you can do to change the situation: sit at the front instead of the back; change your note-taking method. If all else fails, investigate 'lecture capture' options.

2) This could work well with a group assignment, but if it is an individual assignment, be careful that collaboration does not turn into collusion. Also, although group work can be a very positive experience, there are often problems with sharing out the workload and acknowledging everyone's contribution fairly. Furthermore, be aware that it's not always possible to work with people you know and get on with. The reality at university and in the workplace is that you may have to work with anyone, and that you may have to negotiate difficult relationships. Indeed, negotiating relationships is an essential part of teaching.

3) It depends. Can you survive on four hours of sleep? Former UK Prime Minister Margaret Thatcher famously claimed to! But most people cannot. Also, it's worth asking if your mind really does work better at that time or if you've persuaded yourself of this because you like to lie in!

4) There are no easy solutions when it comes to juggling work and family life. You could try to arrange extra childcare to allow you to study in the library for an hour or so before you go home. If this is not a practical option for you, you could attempt to get the TV and phones turned off for a set time (not an easy task!) while the kids do their homework and you study. Another alternative could be to wait until the kids go to bed before you study, but this could affect your alertness the next day.

In the end, the right learning approach for you in a particular situation is whatever gets the best results! The important thing is to be aware of what facilitates learning and what hinders learning for *you*, generally or in a particular situation. Be prepared to abandon unsuccessful study strategies and try out new ones, even if it means venturing out of your comfort zone. Experimentation and trial and error are part of learning and part of life, and these involve taking risks, making mistakes, reflecting on experience, and seeking and accepting feedback and advice. One of the joys of developing as a student or professional is 'the light-bulb moment', where you realise where you are going wrong or what really works for you.

Case studies

Look at the comments below. Could you benefit from any of the strategies these people adopted? Have you had any similar 'light-bulb moments' about your own work and study habits?

1) "I used to get the bus to work, and tried to do some reading for my part-time Master's en route. But it was often hard to concentrate – the bus was crowded and noisy and I worried about missing my stop. Then, to save a bit of money, I started to walk to work – it takes about 30 minutes. I instantly felt better knowing I was doing some exercise and getting some fresh air every day, especially as I was spending so much of my day hunched over a computer. But I became aware of another unexpected advantage. I found that when my brain was free to 'wander', I often started to think about what I'd written the night before, and I was suddenly seeing what I'd written on the page in a different way. Stepping away from the page allowed me to make sense of things, to see how everything hung together, to see new patterns and relationships. I then couldn't wait to get back to the writing and rejig it. Certainly more productive than reading the same paragraph three times on the bus!"

2) "On my computer, I would write a little bit towards my essay, get some ideas down, make some notes for finishing off later. When I was really motivated, I would work for hours uninterrupted but there often came a point when I just stared at the screen and nothing seemed to happen. I could not get my words to make sense. What I learned was that if I left my work at this point (perhaps it was my brain telling me to stop) – for a couple of hours, a day or maybe a week, but not too long – things made much more sense when I went back to them."

Top tips

Mindmaps and MindGenius

If you feel that diagrammatic representations facilitate your learning (ie that you are a 'visual' learner, according to the VAK model (Dunn et al, 1984)), you could find that **mind maps** are useful. Mind maps are an image-centred system for recording and categorising information. If you find mind maps are your thing, you may wish to investigate **MindGenius**, a tool for 'computer-aided thinking'. It allows you to create mind maps on screen in an editable format. It may be particularly useful for students with learning difficulties such as dyslexia. Interfacing with Microsoft Word and PowerPoint means that it can be used to create essays and presentations.

Collaborative learning

The importance and necessity of independent learning has been explained in this chapter. However, universities also value another type of learning very highly: **collaborative learning**. Collaborative learning is an approach to learning that involves '*joint intellectual effort by students, or students and teachers together*' (Smith and MacGregor, 1992, p 1).

There are many ways in which you could be asked to work with your peers at university, including:

- group projects;
- group presentations;
- seminars;
- teaching placements;
- simulated learning, via mock classrooms or role play, for example;
- peer marking, eg marking the work of your fellow students as a way of exploring task requirements.

Libraries and learning commons often have group study facilities to accommodate this important aspect of learning at university.

Reflection

1) Think of some of the advantages that could come from working collaboratively with others.
2) Think of some occasions when you have been part of a group.
3) Was it a positive or negative experience? Below are some suggested positive outcomes of group work and collaboration. Did you experience any of these?

- having a sense of being part of a learning community;
- feeling supported;
- achieving more than you might be able to alone;
- hearing diverse and stimulating perspectives and experiences;
- learning different ways to do things;
- clarifying your own ideas through discussion;
- learning to make a point effectively;
- acquiring interpersonal skills;
- having the opportunity to take on different roles;
- acquiring leadership skills;
- gaining confidence;
- learning to deal with being challenged and criticised;
- socialising;
- preparing for the practices of the workplace.

Collaboration in teaching

The Teachers' Standards (DfE, 2013) describe teachers' professional responsibilities as follows:

8. Fulfil wider professional responsibilities
   - make a positive contribution to the wider life and ethos of the school

   - develop effective professional relationships with colleagues, knowing how and when to draw on advice and specialist support

   - deploy support staff effectively

   - take responsibility for improving teaching through appropriate professional development, responding to advice and feedback from colleagues

   - communicate effectively with parents with regard to pupils' achievements and well-being

Collaboration in action

Independent learning and collaborative learning are by no means mutually exclusive. Students working together in groups or teams will most often be working autonomously from the lecturers, while at the same time drawing on their collective knowledge and resources to complete a task, solve a problem etc. Furthermore, group work will often involve both group and individual elements. Figure 2.2 represents the possible dynamics of a group presentation, where the group has responsibility for the ideas, and how they are organised and represented visually (eg through PowerPoint), and the individual has the responsibility both to contribute to group work and to deliver part of the presentation directly to an audience. It is important to understand this dynamic. If for example, you just focus on getting your own bit right, your mark could still be affected by weaknesses in the general organisation of ideas. Similarly, it is mainly the group, not the individual, who will usually be given credit for the brilliant idea you focus on in your own part. The group can also provide constructive input on each other's individual performance during presentation practice. Sometimes the marking system will include separate marks for the group and the individual (though these are often hard to separate completely – a good idea is better if it is conveyed to the audience in an engaging way by an individual presenter, and a group presentation will be more successful if its constituent parts are as good as they can be).

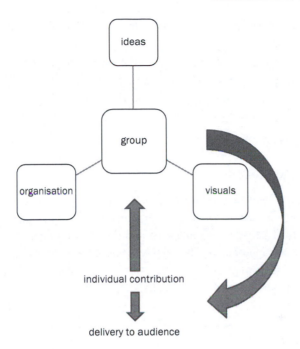

Figure 2.2: Group presentations

Other group tasks will work in a different way. In a group writing project, for example, you will have to work together to:

- identify and distribute reading/research tasks fairly and efficiently;
- find productive ways of sharing information and using it to devise a structure and framework for the written report;
- decide if you will have individuals writing different parts of the report, or if you will try some collaborative writing activities;
- determine how the whole thing comes together;
- format and proofread the report – discovering who in the group has these important skills is a key task.

Important qualities in group work

Participants in group work require certain qualities and skills, eg:

- being a good listener;
- being ready to learn from others;
- being confident about what you have to offer;
- getting your message across;
- giving and receiving constructive criticism;
- giving and accepting support from others;

- being aware of group dynamics so that you can help the group 'gel' and avoid serious problems;
- identifying the roles that you and others can play to be effective group members and so get the most out of all members of the group;
- putting the needs of the group before your own while also using the experience for personal development;
- being self-aware and reflective so that you can improve your collaborative skills.

Managing conflict

Group work, by its very nature, often provokes conflict. While it is probably safe to say that a degree of conflict is a normal part of group work, it is of course necessary to manage it in some way. In the early part of your studies, lecturers may provide support to facilitate the way you work together, but as you progress, this type of facilitation will probably decrease or disappear. You will be relied upon to find your own solutions to challenges that arise.

Reflection

1) What kind of conflicts do you think may arise in group work? Have you experienced any of these things? How did you respond?

2) Here are some issues which commonly arise. How might you manage or resolve these issues?

- some students not 'pulling their weight', leaving others to feel the mark awarded to the group is affected by an individual's poor performance;

- some students not taking the task seriously – not turning up for meetings or shirking their responsibilities;

- some students dominating, not allowing participation from the whole group – especially quieter students – resulting in some students feeling left out;

- some students relying on lecturers to resolve conflict;

- some students forming cliques or even bullying other students.

Discussion: managing conflict

There is no one answer to any of these problems, but the following may help.

What the group can do:

- create and maintain channels of communication (meetings, email, Facebook, WhatsApp);
- set some 'ground rules' (communication, attendance, punctuality, turn-taking, phone etiquette, role allocation etc);
- include everyone in the group and be careful not to discriminate for any reason;

- find a way of negotiating with each other in a calm, sensitive and respectful way;
- be clear about the purpose of each meeting and the tasks you are involved with – think about using an agenda;
- in meetings, arrange the physical environment so that everyone can see and hear everyone else;
- manage negativity – encourage the discussion of solutions rather than just focusing on problems;
- spend some time investigating each other's strengths (PowerPoint, proofreading, communication within the group, understanding statistics etc), so that the workload can be more effectively distributed – rotate roles if this seems fairer;
- keep a record of what decisions are taken and who is responsible for what;
- create a relaxed atmosphere in meetings – a plate of biscuits might help!

What you can do:

CROSS REFERENCE

Communication Skills, Chapter 2, Participating in seminars and meetings

- remember that if the group succeeds, so do you, so it is worth taking a positive approach;
- be prepared for meetings; do what you have been asked to do; if you weren't able to do something, apologise and explain;
- be kind, helpful and encouraging to others, especially if they are struggling. This is a good thing to do *per se*, but remember that people also learn a lot by explaining things to others;
- adopt positive body language when others are talking – make eye contact, smile etc;
- respond to others with affirmation, comments, questions etc when appropriate;
- when you speak, acknowledge and build on what others have said where appropriate;
- be gentle and constructive in your criticisms – avoid nastiness and blaming people;
- if you don't understand, ask – it is likely that others are in the same boat;
- you may wish to look at some of the information provided by ACAS (the Advisory, Conciliation and Arbitration Service; see, for example ACAS, 2014), an independent body whose remit is to improve relations between employers and employees.

Summary

This chapter has explored some of the strategies available to you as you strive to become an effective learner, meet the expectations of university study and achieve your own personal goals. It has discussed various approaches to learning, with the aim of encouraging you to identify and explore approaches which might work well for you, without limiting your options. Finally, it has examined the role of collaborative learning in HE.

References

ACAS (2014) *Managing Conflict at Work* [online]. Available at: www.acas.org.uk/media/pdf/j/o/Managing-conflict-at-work-advisory-booklet.pdf (accessed 16 February 2018).

Devine, T (1987) *Teaching Study Skills*. Newton, MA: Allyn and Bacon.

DfE (2013) *Teachers' Standards: Guidance for School Leaders, School Staff and Governing Bodies*. London: DfE.

Dunn, R, Dunn, K and Price, G (1984) *Learning Style Inventory*. Lawrence, KS: Price Systems.

Fleming, N and Mills, C (1992) Not another Inventory, Rather a Catalyst for Action. *To Improve the Academy*, paper 246 [online]. Available at: http://digitalcommons.unl.edu/podimproveacad/246/ (accessed 16 February 2018).

Honey, P and Mumford, A (1982) *Manual of Learning Styles*. London: P. Honey.

Jenkins, A (2009) *Research-Teaching Linkages: Enhancing Graduate Attributes* [online]. Available at: www.enhancementthemes.ac.uk/docs/publications/research-teaching-linkages-enhancing-graduate-attributes-overview.pdf?sfvrsn=20 (accessed 11 February 2018).

Marks, N (2014) Guardian Readers Reveal What Makes Them Happy at Work. *The Guardian* [online]. Available at: www.theguardian.com/sustainable-business/happy-work-what-makes-you (accessed 16 February 2018).

Smith, B and Macgregor, J (1992) What is Collaborative Learning? In Goodsell, A, Maher, M, Tinto, V, Smith, B and MacGregor, J (eds) *Collaborative Learning: A Source Book for Higher Education*. University Park, PA: National Centre on Postsecondary Teaching, Learning and Assessment, Pennsylvania State University.

Willingham, D, Hughes, E and Dobolyi, D (2015) The Scientific Status of Learning Style Theories. *Teaching of Psychology*, 42(3): 266–71.

Chapter 3
Becoming a member of your academic and professional community

Learning outcomes

After reading this chapter you will:

- have gained an understanding of the values and principles which underpin your discipline and the wider HE community;

- have gained an understanding of some of the practices and conventions of your discipline and the wider HE community;

- have developed your understanding of how knowledge is developed in HE;

- have begun to gain an understanding of how knowledge and language relate to each other;

- have gained an understanding of the concept of 'graduate attributes'.

A university can be seen as an 'academic community', a group of academic practitioners (people who teach, learn and do research) who share a particular way of thinking about the world. This chapter explores the challenges that you might face as you strive to become a member of this community and enter the discipline of teaching. This chapter also introduces the concept of 'graduate attributes' and discusses their relevance to your studies.

Joining the academy

It is notable that Becher (1989), in a landmark study of universities and those who cultivate knowledge across the many existing disciplines, refers to the different groups found in universities as 'tribes', with their own cultures, or 'territories'. Becoming a student means joining one of these 'tribes' and functioning within its 'territory'. This can be a real challenge. As with all social interactions, there are certain codes of behaviour, or 'rules', that need to be followed. What's more, although some of these codes or rules may be explicit, others can appear to be rather hidden or obscure: rules regarding the payment of fees, or the return of library books are usually clearly signalled and easy to understand, but 'rules' on how to address your lecturers or even how to reference academic sources can be harder to decipher – and are often understood through trial and error. Moreover, these are things which often vary across disciplines and institutions, and even according to individual preferences.

Case studies

Think about the situations below. What do you think would be the best way to proceed in each case?

1) You are going to meet your academic adviser for the first time. You've heard that people use first names rather than surnames and titles in British universities, but this is very different from your country and you don't really feel comfortable with it.

2) You need to email a lecturer for the first time and you are not sure of the most appropriate way of wording or structuring it.

3) You have been instructed to write 'formally' in your essays but you thought you were already doing this!

4) You have been told that your work is not 'critical' but do not really understand what this means.

5) You have been informed that 'plagiarism' is a very serious issue and it has made you feel very nervous about using too much information from books and articles.

Discussion of case studies

CROSS REFERENCE

Communication Skills

1) It is true that it is common to address lecturers, and even professors, by their first names in universities in the UK. This can seem rather strange, especially for students who come from cultures where a more formal acknowledgement of status and hierarchy is expected. What's more, it can cause confusion, because the use of first names can imply the absence of a hierarchy, and this is not really the case: while there is usually a fairly relaxed, collaborative relationship between students and academic staff in UK universities, this does not mean that anything goes! It might be a good idea in this case to start by using the lecturer's title (Dr Gonzalez, Professor Mason); they may well ask you to call them by their first name from that point on.

2) Use a fairly standard, semi-formal email such as the ones below. It is common in this type of email communication to use certain fixed phrases which can be reused on other occasions; the emails below contain some of these phrases.

CROSS REFERENCE

Academic Writing and Referencing, Chapter 4, Language in use, style

> Dear Dr Jones,
>
> I would like to meet with you briefly to discuss my teaching placement. Could you please let me know when your office hours are?
>
> Thank you in advance for your assistance.
>
> Best wishes,
> Karin

Dear Professor Coppinger,

Please find attached my report on a child's reading progress, following our visit to Sherburn Primary last week.

Many thanks for your advice on this assessment.

Regards,
Maria

Over time, the emails may become less formal ('Hi' instead of 'Dear'; first names instead of surnames; 'Best' instead of 'Best wishes'), but you should maintain a formal tone if you are at all unsure.

3) You could perhaps arrange to meet with the lecturer who gave you the feedback to find out what it is exactly that is too informal. Are you using conversational words such as 'actually'? Are you using personal language like 'I really think' or 'you should realise'? Is the text too 'chatty' and lacking in structure? You could also consult a textbook on academic writing (eg Baily, 2014; Bottomley, 2014; Swales and Feak, 2012), or find out about the resources in your university. Most universities have library resources with information on academic writing, and most have in-sessional writing classes where you can receive expert guidance. You may be able to book a 'writing tutorial', sometimes called a 'writing consultation', which will provide you with personalised help, either using a piece of writing you are currently working on, or one that has been returned to you with a mark and comments from a lecturer. In the latter case, the writing tutor will be able to help you understand why you received the mark and feedback you did. Also, remember that good dictionaries label informal and slang words, so always check if you are at all unsure; if you've never used a word before, you should always check it in the dictionary and look at typical examples of the word in use.

CROSS REFERENCE

Academic Writing and Referencing, Appendix 1, English language references

4) Criticality is a difficult abstract concept. Being critical involves analysing, interpreting and evaluating information and ideas. It requires an active reading of the literature to discern relationships and patterns. It necessitates using ideas and evidence from the literature to support and develop your own argument. Some students may have academic skills relating to criticality when they start university but many do not; universities usually understand this and often work with first-year students to help them develop the critical reading and writing skills they need in subsequent years.

CROSS REFERENCE

Chapter 4, Critical thinking

5) Plagiarism is indeed a serious issue, but it is one which is often misunderstood. It is certainly not the same thing as making a lot of references to sources, which is actually a very good thing! Problems can arise for international students because of differences between how different academic cultures treat sources. Issues also sometimes surface if students do not have the confidence to allow their own voice to come to the fore in an essay. Again, it might be a good idea to seek out writing support from the library or in-sessional writing classes and tutorials. Also, many universities offer VLE courses on 'academic malpractice' which will help you to understand what the issues are and how to avoid plagiarism and other forms of malpractice.

CROSS REFERENCE

Critical Thinking Skills

Top tips

CROSS REFERENCE

Academic Writing and Referencing, Chapter 3, Referring to sources

Being informed

Universities generally have an obligation to say what they expect from you, and what you can expect from them in return. Indeed, you might find these expectations enshrined in a formal document such as an 'Educational Contract' or 'Student Charter', or they might be embedded in a course handbook. These documents (or links to them) are usually given to students in the first week or so of starting university. As an adult learner, it is up to you to read these documents. If you are unsure of anything, it is also up to you to ask questions.

Academic principles, pursuits and practices

Joining the academic community will be easier if you are fully aware of why universities exist and what it is that the people in them believe.

Teaching, research and knowledge

The two pillars of university life are **research** and **teaching**. Universities have strong beliefs about how research should be conducted and how **teaching and learning** should occur. This affects, among other things, how students are expected to engage in learning and how they will be assessed.

CROSS REFERENCE

Chapter 4, Critical thinking

Universities are committed to the pursuit and advancement of **knowledge**. This knowledge is presented, discussed and tested through specific '*communicative events*' with a particular shared purpose. These academic '*genres*' (Swales, 1990, p 58) include lectures, research papers, essays and exams, each characterised by particular content and conventions.

CROSS REFERENCE

Academic Writing and Referencing, Chapter 2, Referring to sources

As a university student, it is not enough to simply acquire and demonstrate knowledge; university study requires the acquisition of a set of intellectual skills that become increasingly complex as you move through your academic career. In your first year, the emphasis will largely be on achieving and demonstrating **understanding** of concepts and theories in your field; in subsequent years, this understanding will be need to be underpinned by **criticality**; postgraduate (Master's or Doctoral) level studies will almost certainly expect you to perform an **intellectual synthesis** of theories and concepts relevant to your field (pulling these theories and concepts together to create a broad understanding and generate new theories and concepts).

In order to be able to engage with knowledge in your field in a meaningful way, it is important that you understand what knowledge is and how it typically advances in academia.

Task

Look at the following real-life examples. What do they tell you about knowledge?

Teaching reading through phonics

Johnston and Watson (2003, 2004, 2005) are two influential researchers who promote systematic synthetic phonics. They conducted a research study in Clackmannanshire Scotland, implementing a phonics intervention programme with groups of children in the early stages of learning to read. They had a number of intervention groups, with each group being taught using different approaches to learning to read. They concluded that "the synthetic phonics approach, as part of the reading curriculum, is more effective that the analytical phonics approach" (Johnston and Watson, 2005: 9). It was this report that was cited by Rose (2006) and was significant in his conclusions and recommendations about the teaching of reading and phonics. The research methodology and so the robustness of the findings has been contested, and in reaching your own conclusions it is useful to read widely. Wyse and Styles (2007) provided a detailed critique of the study which is then countered and critiqued in a series of articles in the journal *Literacy* (2007). These articles 'play out' the debates surrounding the research and provide a good starting point for analysis of research evidence.

A further area of debate surrounds the teaching of synthetic phonics to able readers and in particular children who begin school as readers. Davis (2013) challenges the research evidence that has been used to promote synthetic phonics. He challenges the assumption that successful phonics teaching can automatically be equated with the successful teaching of reading. Reading, he claims is not simply about mastering letter sound correspondences but is about the making of meaning and that whilst phonics can help some children on their journey to becoming readers it is not an approach that supports all children and in particular, the able reader.

(Adapted from Waugh, D, Carter, J and Desmond, C (2015)
Lessons in Teaching Phonics. London: Sage.)

The example above should help you recognise that much remains unknown in academia, and that knowledge is usually advanced in small steps, often with many wrong turns along the way. For this reason, there is a certain tolerance of uncertainty and ambiguity, and an acceptance of the idea that the more you learn, the less straightforward things tend to become. Scholarship is advanced in part by researchers approaching the literature critically, and thus identifying and exploring **'gaps'** or problems in the current knowledge. The research they do can be **quantitative** (research including 'quantities', ie numbers) or **qualitative** (research concerned with 'qualities', ie experiences, feelings, perceptions etc). In education and a number of other disciplines, **mixed methods** research – research that combines quantitative and qualitative research – is becoming more common. Research findings are usually presented (or 'disseminated') in research reports in academic journals, and you will be required to read these as part of your studies.

CROSS
REFERENCE

*Academic
Writing and
Referencing*

Advanced skills

Research reports

A postgraduate education dissertation or thesis, and sometimes an undergraduate research dissertation, may be a report on a piece of research you have carried out. Research dissertations in teaching usually follow an **IMRAD** structure.

This approach to writing about research can be summarised in simple terms as follows:

- **I**ntroduction – what was your research and why did you do it?

- **M**ethod – how did you do it?

- **R**esults – what did you find out?

- **D**iscussion – what does it all mean?

An **I**ntroduction highlights a 'gap' or a problem that your research will address, together with its context and background. It tells the reader why the research is important, and prepares the ground for your study by presenting a **literature review**, that is to say, a critical analysis and evaluation of the current scholarship on the topic, out of which your own argument has emerged. The way you write your introduction is very important, as this is your opportunity to grab the attention of your reader and persuade them of the importance and the logic of your argument.

A **M**ethodology details the way you go about collecting and analysing your data. Your method should be presented in such a way that it can be easily replicated by others. Scholars (or assessors) will scrutinise this to help them judge the validity of your findings.

A research dissertation must include a summary and analysis of the **R**esults. **Figures** and **Tables** may be particularly useful tools in this section.

A research dissertation ends with a **D**iscussion of the meaning, significance and implications of your findings. This section will almost certainly contain a discussion of the limitations of the study, and possibly recommendations for further study.

There may also be a **Conclusion**, which usually outlines the implications for teaching. A research report also includes an **Abstract** at the beginning which summarises the study and the main findings. The report concludes with a list of **References** and any **Appendices**.

Values, beliefs and academic integrity

Every community has its own culture, and universities are no different. Academic culture is characterised by particular **values** and **beliefs**. Universities value, among other things, **independent thinking**, **intellectual curiosity** and **freedom of speech**. They believe in **evidence-based** enquiry and activity. They maintain that systems and processes should be **rigorous** and **transparent**. They promote **objectivity** and **criticality**. Of course, all of these are ideals, and like all ideals, they are not always achieved – but they are aspired to. All members of the academic community, including you, play a part in meeting these aspirations.

Academic integrity refers to the moral principles aspired to by universities. One way that universities seek to promote academic integrity is through the use of **reputable sources** and accurate attribution through **referencing**; they consequently see **plagiarism** as one of the most serious attacks on their culture and values.

Another important aspect of academic integrity is **ethical awareness**. This means behaving according to a strict moral code. The implications of this with regard to teaching are discussed later in this chapter, when the Teachers' Standards are discussed.

CROSS REFERENCE

Academic Writing and Referencing, Chapter 3, Referring to sources

Communication

Academics and students are expected to communicate their knowledge and ideas in a clear, professional way, following the conventions of their discipline. This is particularly the case in those disciplines – including teaching – that involve significant interaction with the public.

CROSS REFERENCE

Academic Writing and Referencing, Chapter 3, Coherence in texts and arguments

Academic phrasebank

Like any community, the academic community has a shared language. While specialist knowledge and terminology varies across disciplines, there are certain things that all members of the academic community do (as discussed in the last section), and they all make use of certain set phrases and structures to do it. At the University of Manchester, a 'bank' of such phrases and structures has been developed through the analysis of academic texts. These are categorised according to functions, ie the things academics *do* with language. Some common categories (related to the ideas discussed in this chapter) and phrases/structures are explored in the task below. Note the *non-committal* tone of many of the phrases, which reflects the many *uncertainties* surrounding knowledge in academia.

CROSS REFERENCE

Academic Writing and Referencing, Chapter 4, Language in use, Clarity

Task

Match each of the functions (numbered) below with a set of phrases and structures (identified by letters A, B, C, etc).

Functions:

1) Identifying knowledge gaps
2) Putting forward an argument
3) Providing evidence

4) Making reference to sources

5) Evaluating sources

6) Acknowledging uncertainty, contradiction and ambiguity

7) Explaining implications

Phrases and structures:

A _____

In his seminal text, Potter explored the social implications of …

The pioneering work of Gonzalez remains crucial to our understanding of …

The article provides a valuable insight into …

The main weaknesses of the study lie in its failure to …

B _____

There has been a great deal of research into this area.

Previous studies have established that …

Suvaris argues that …

While acknowledging the need for further research into this area, McVey concludes that …

C _____

The data supports this.

The evidence to date suggests that …

This can be seen most obviously in the case of …

In a recent study, it was found that …

D _____

To date, there has been little research into the issue of …

The effects of this remain unclear.

What is not yet clear is …

Little attention has been paid to …

E _____

Taken as a whole, these results suggest …

These findings suggest a role for …

This study strengthens the case for …

The implications of these findings are clear.

F _____

However, taking into consideration the small sample size, …

Correlation, of course, does not equal causality.

The data must be interpreted with caution, as …

It is important to allow for bias in the responses due to …

See the website for more examples: www.phrasebank.manchester.ac.uk/

The education community

Teaching practice is underpinned by essential knowledge and values, developed over time, and represented in recent years in the Teachers' Standards.

Historical landmarks in education

As in any discipline, knowledge and values have emerged out of particular landmarks in the history of education, some of which are briefly outlined below.

Table 3.1: Landmarks in the history of teaching and school education in the United Kingdom post-Second World War

DATE	KEY EVENT OR LEGISLATION
1944	The *Butler Act* established the structure of the post-war system of state education and included selection at 11 for secondary education in secondary modern, technical or grammar schools.
1964	The Labour manifesto promised to abolish selection.
1967	The Plowden Report, *Children and Their Primary Schools*, promoted child-centred education. It was criticised by traditionalists.
1973	The school leaving age was raised to 16.
1974	The William Tyndale Affair: chaos at a primary school led to the 'Black Papers' and helped pave the way for Jim Callaghan's 1976 Ruskin Speech (see below).
1975	The Bullock Report, *A Language for Life*, was a major report on the teaching of English.
1976	The *Education Act* gave the Secretary of State the power to ask Local Education Authorities (LEAs) to plan for non-selective (comprehensive) secondary education. This was repealed by the Conservatives in 1979.
1976	Jim Callaghan gave a speech at Ruskin College on 18 October in which he questioned some current practices in education. This began 'The Great Debate' about education.
1978	The Warnock Report, *Special Educational Needs*, looked at provision for children and young people with special needs.
1980	The 1980 *Education Act* introduced the assisted places scheme which provided public money for children to go to private schools, gave parents greater powers on governing bodies and over admissions, and removed LEAs' obligation to provide school milk and meals.
1982	The Cockcroft Report, *Mathematics Counts*, was a major report on the teaching of maths.
1984	The Council for the Accreditation of Teacher Education (CATE) was established to set standards for initial teacher training courses.

1988	The 1988 *Education Reform Act* established the National Curriculum, a testing regime and Local Management of Schools (LMS), which transferred some responsibility for managing schools' finances from local authorities to schools.
1989	The Elton Report, *Discipline in Schools,* was published.
1991	The Parents' Charter: this gave parents the right to information about schools and their performance.
1992	The 1992 *Education (Schools) Act* introduced arrangements for the inspection of schools and led to the creation of Ofsted (Office for Standards in Education).
1998	The National Literacy Strategy was launched in September. For the first time, teachers were given strict guidelines for organising lessons (literacy hours).
1999	The National Numeracy Strategy was launched in September.
2000	City academies: David Blunkett announced the government's intention to create a network of academies – effectively private schools paid for by the state.
2003	Green Paper, *Every Child Matters*: this was Labour's attempt to take a holistic view of children and their life chances, and it led to the 2004 *Children Act.*
2006	The *Primary National Strategy* introduced a new Primary Framework for literacy and mathematics.
2008	The *Education and Skills Act* raised the education leaving age to 18; Key Stage 3 SATs were effectively abolished.
2008	The free schools policy was announced by Michael Gove (Shadow Education Secretary) as a means of allowing schools to be set up outside local authority control.
2010	The *Academies Act* allowed significant and rapid expansion of academies.
2013	DfE *Teachers' Standards* were introduced and became the standards against which teachers were assessed. These applied to both trainee and practising teachers.
2013	DfE *Revision of National Curriculum*. Revisions included a much stronger emphasis on grammar, spelling and punctuation in primary schools.

Reflection

Which of the events or developments in Table 3.1 do you think have had the most impact on education today? Why?

Graduate attributes

Belonging to a particular community entails developing in a way that is valued by that community. UK universities have stated a commitment to fostering certain attributes which it is believed students should possess when they graduate. These **graduate attributes** have been defined as '*the skills, knowledge and abilities of university graduates, beyond disciplinary knowledge, which are applicable to a range of contexts*' (Barrie, 2004, p 262). They relate to the following areas:

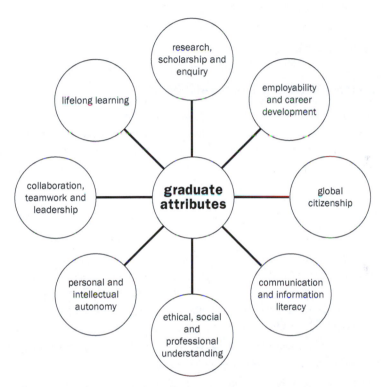

Figure 3.1: Graduate attributes (adapted from Hounsell, 2011, pp 2–3)

Reflection

Do you agree that these are the most important attributes that a graduate should demonstrate?

Do you think there are any important attributes missing from the list?

Task

Which graduate attributes could be developed in the following activities? How?

1) Giving a group presentation
2) Completing a dissertation

3) Contributing to an internet forum on educational issues

4) Becoming familiar with the Teachers' Standards

5) Finding and subsequently attending a library workshop on developing PowerPoint skills

6) Actively managing your online presence (Facebook, Twitter, Instagram, LinkedIn etc)

7) Carefully proofreading your essay

8) Reading a quality newspaper (paper or online) on a regular basis

9) Becoming a course representative in your department

10) Learning a language

Discussion: applying graduate attributes

1) Giving a group presentation involves collaborative preparation and planning, working in teams with other students. It might also be necessary for you to take on a leadership role if you have knowledge or experience which others do not (*collaboration, teamwork and leadership*). As teamwork and leadership are highly valued in the workplace, you will be enhancing your own employability (*employability and career development*). In order to prepare your presentation, you will need to draw on and develop your research and communication skills (*research, scholarship and enquiry; communication and information literacy*).

2) Completing a dissertation requires autonomy (*personal and intellectual autonomy*) and advanced research skills (*research, scholarship and enquiry*), including command of technological resources (*communication and information literacy*). Academic writing is a key communication skill (*communication and information literacy*) which will also prepare you for formal communication in the workplace, thus enhancing your employability (*employability and career development*).

3) Contributing to an internet forum on educational issues is a form of collaboration (*collaboration, teamwork and leadership*) and a way of exploring social and professional understanding (*ethical, social and professional understanding*). It also develops a particular set of communication skills related to social networking which could extend to a global scale (*communication and information literacy; global citizenship*).

4) Becoming familiar with the Teachers' Standards is primarily a way of extending professional understanding for academic and workplace purposes (*ethical, social and professional understanding; employability and career development*).

5) Finding and subsequently attending a library workshop on developing PowerPoint skills displays personal autonomy (*personal and intellectual autonomy*) and a commitment to improving your communication skills (*communication and information literacy; lifelong learning*). PowerPoint is also a skill valued by employers (*employability and career development*).

6) Actively managing your online presence (Facebook, Twitter, Instagram, LinkedIn etc) allows you to be in control of how you are viewed by potential employers

and colleagues (*communication and information literacy, employability and career development*).

7) Carefully proofreading your essay indicates a commitment to developing your written communication skills (*communication and information literacy*). This will be valued in academia and in the workplace (*employability and career development*).

8) Reading a quality newspaper (paper or online) on a regular basis can be a way of keeping up to date with social and global issues (*ethical, social and professional understanding*), which can in turn help you to understand and respond to workplace issues (*employability and career development*).

9) Becoming a course representative in your academic department can help you build on your communication and leadership skills (*communication and information literacy, collaboration, teamwork and leadership*). This is something that might catch the eye of a prospective employer if included on your CV (*employability and career development*).

10) Learning a language is a way of achieving cultural understanding, and of enhancing your skill set in an increasingly internationalised workplace (*global citizenship; lifelong learning*).

Top tips

Standing out to prospective employers

Be sure to add activities like those discussed above to your CV, as the graduate attributes they demonstrate are of great interest to employers. Evidence of such attributes could make you stand out in a competitive employment market.

Summary

This chapter has explored the ways in which you can become a member of your academic community. It has discussed the values and principles which underpin university life and the foundations of education and teaching. It has detailed some of the practices and conventions which govern both academic life, and teacher education and practice. It has also introduced the concept of graduate attributes, and examined their importance in terms of employability.

References

Academic Phrasebank [online]. Available at: www.phrasebank.manchester.ac.uk/ (accessed 16 February 2018).

Baily, S (2014) *Academic Writing: A Handbook for International Students*. 4th ed. Abingdon: Routledge.

Barrie, S (2004) A Research-based Approach to Generic Graduate Attributes Policy. *Higher Education Research & Development*, 23(3): 261–75.

Becher, T (1989) *Academic Tribes and Territories: Intellectual Enquiry and the Culture of Disciplines*. Buckingham: Society for Research in Higher Education and Open University Press.

Bottomley, J (2014) *Academic Writing for International Students of Science*. Abingdon: Routledge.

DfE (2013) *Teachers' Standards: Guidance for School Leaders, School Staff and Governing Bodies*. London: DfE. This document is available for download at www.gov.uk/government/publications.

Gillard, D (2011) *Education in England: A Brief History*. Available at: www.educationengland.org.uk/history (accessed 17 February 2018).

Hounsell, D (2011) *Graduates for the 21st Century: Integrating the Enhancement Themes*. Glasgow: The Quality Assurance Agency for Higher Education, pp 2–3.

Swales, J (1990) *Genre Analysis*. Cambridge: Cambridge University Press.

Swales, J and Feak, C (2012) *Academic Writing for Graduate Students: Essential Tasks and Skills*. 3rd ed. Michigan: Michigan ELT.

Chapter 4
Critical thinking

Learning outcomes

After reading this chapter you will:

- understand what is meant by the term 'critical';

- have gained an understanding of what it means to think critically;

- have developed a critical approach to learning and the use of resources;

- have acquired some strategies for reading critically;

- have acquired some strategies for writing, and presenting work, critically.

Critical thinking lies at the heart of academic life and is essential for academic success. As a university student, you will be expected to take a critical approach to all your learning activities and assessment tasks. This chapter introduces the concept of critical thinking and explores its application in the acquisition and reporting of information and ideas, as well as in teaching practice. The ideas in this chapter are discussed in further detail in the *Critical Thinking* book in the Critical Study Skills series.

What is critical thinking?

You will encounter the word 'critical' frequently in university life: you may be asked to *write critically* in an essay, or to *critically review* a journal article; you may receive feedback on an essay which says it is not *critical* enough, that you need to adopt a more *critical approach*; there may be modules on your course with titles such as *Critical Thinking*, and the course descriptions of other modules may mention the importance of *criticality*, *critical reading skills* and *critical writing skills*. It is clear that being *critical* is important in academic life. But what do academics mean when they use this word?

Reflection

Look at the entry for 'critical' in the *Chambers 21st Century Dictionary*. Which of the definitions do you think most reflects the way academics would usually use this word? Which, for you, is the most 'normal' use in day-to-day life?

critical /ˈkrɪtɪkəl/ ▷ *adj* **1** fault-finding; disapproving. **2** relating to a critic or criticism. **3** involving analysis and assessment. **4** relating to a crisis; decisive; crucial. **5** urgent; vital. **6** said of a patient: so ill or seriously injured as to be at risk of dying. **7** *physics* denoting a state, level or value at which there is a significant change in the properties of a system □ *critical mass* □ *critical temperature*. **8** *nuclear physics* said of a fissionable material, a nuclear reactor, etc: having reached the point at which a nuclear chain reaction is self-sustaining. ● **critically** *adverb*. ● **criticality** *noun*. ● **criticalness** *noun*.

When you are asked at university to do something in a 'critical' way, it is normally the third use, involving 'analysis and assessment' (Chambers), which is meant. Other dictionary definitions include the related terms 'evaluation' (Oxford Dictionaries), or 'judgement' (Merriam-Webster). This use of the word is different from the most common use of the word in everyday life, ie 'fault-finding' or 'disapproving'; however, negative judgements can of course form part of general evaluation – a critical review of an article will discuss weaknesses as well as strengths. Criticising in this sense is certainly part of critical thinking, but it is not central.

Since academics frequently use the term 'critical' in conjunction with 'analyse' and 'evaluate', or imply these things in their use of the word 'critical', it is important to understand precisely what they mean by these words. To explore this, it is helpful to step outside the academic world and consider for a moment your wider everyday life.

Reflection

Consider the questions below.

1) Why did you decide to become a teacher?

2) How did you choose a particular university for your studies?

3) Where do you get your news about the world? Why?

4) Who is your favourite writer? Why?

5) Is your diet healthy? Why/why not?

6) How did you choose what to wear this morning?

In order to answer the reflection questions, you had to **analyse** by examining certain things in a detailed and systematic way, breaking them down into their constituent parts. You might have:

- looked at a range of different occupations in terms of how interesting they appear, the knowledge and skills required, and the degree to which they match your own personality and skills;
- categorised universities according to region, type or reputation;
- distinguished newspapers or news websites according to their readability and/or political allegiances;
- identified the characteristics which distinguish a particular writer;
- assigned foods to different groups such as proteins, carbohydrates and fats;
- identified typical weather in the region in which you live.

The questions also require you to **evaluate**, ie *to make judgements*. You may do this to some extent on a personal, subjective level:

- you may feel you have a vocation to be a teacher;
- you may have chosen your university partly because you like a particular city or have family commitments there;
- your personal politics are likely to influence your choice of news outlet;
- your interest in particular topics and your taste in writing style will determine which authors appeal to you;
- your sense of individual style may influence the way you dress.

However, you might also base your judgements on **objective criteria** and **independent evidence** such as published university league tables, established scientific consensus on nutrition, or the evidence-based predictions of trained meteorologists ('weather scientists').

CROSS REFERENCE

Stance

Critical analysis and evaluation enables you to provide **valid reasons** for your judgements and the decisions based on them, and this is a very important part of critical academic discourse. Instead of stating 'I believe such-and-such', or 'I just know such-and-such to be right', in critical academic discourse, you are required to provide an **evidenced-based rationale** for your views and beliefs.

There is no doubt that critical thinking is a difficult, abstract concept, but, as you can see, it is clearly not something mysterious or peculiar to universities. The examples you have reflected on show that critical thinking is in no way disconnected from everyday life: people use their critical faculties every day to form opinions and make decisions. The challenge for you as a new university student is to be aware of your existing, hopefully well-formed and well-practised critical faculties, and to apply them to a new academic context. Of course, there is always room to learn and develop, and being a university student will provide you with a unique opportunity to refine and extend your critical thinking skills, and, crucially, to demonstrate them in your educational studies and assessments. The advanced critical thinking skills you develop at university are themselves transferable: you will go on to apply them in teaching practice and many other areas of life.

The critical thinker

Reflection

Below are some adjectives which could describe a critical thinker:

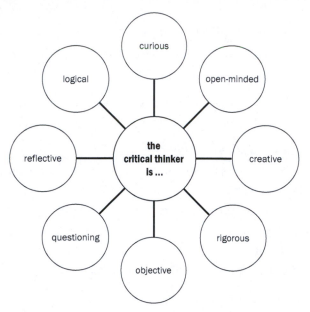

Figure 4.1: Qualities of the critical thinker

1) In what way do you think each of these qualities makes a person critical?
2) Try to think of a recent example in your family, study or work life when you demonstrated (or failed to demonstrate!) each of these qualities.
3) Which of these qualities is reflected in the following?

   - Checking facts and claims in an article with reliable independent sources

   - Considering issues or problems from different angles

   - Gathering facts and ideas from a number of different sources and comparing them

   - Comparing contrasting viewpoints

   - Finding up-to-date examples which support or challenge particular viewpoints

Critical thinking in universities

Critical thinking underpins the development of **knowledge** in universities. Your lecturers at university are also scholars engaged in the advancement of knowledge, and part of their job is to put forward **ideas** about what is going on in the world.

These ideas come about in many ways: they often arise by means of previous work conducted on the subject by other scholars; they may come from direct observation of the world; they may be the result of a 'hunch' a person has (though even hunches usually owe something to previous work done by others – no one works in a vacuum!). In academia, these ideas are usually termed **theories** or **hypotheses**. Unlike facts, these ideas are not certain, and they must be investigated and tested through formal **research** if they are to have a chance of being accepted by the academic community. A particular theory or hypothesis gives rise to a **research question**, which scholars investigate, finding **evidence** along the way to support their ideas. Scholars present their research in a variety of ways, but the main vehicle is the **academic journal**. Scholars trust journal articles because, unlike some other sources, notably the internet, the research articles in them are critically reviewed by other respected scholars, ie they are said to be **peer reviewed**. However, this does not mean that readers can automatically accept the findings and conclusions put forward in journal articles: they must still review the ideas and evidence put forward *critically* to make sure they are credible.

As one scholar puts forward an idea or theory, it is more than likely that another will put forward an alternative one. They may do this because they view the world in a different way, or because they spot 'holes' in the theories of others. The latter situation is not as negative as it might sound. In Chapter 3, you learned that knowledge tends to advance in small steps; it does not suddenly appear, fully and perfectly formed!

Every new theory generates healthy debate, which is necessary to make sure that ideas are rigorously tested. Much of this debate is conducted through academic journals, but conferences and other platforms play a part. The debate tends to be 'won' by the side that has the most substantive and convincing portfolio of evidence or the one whose arguments best fit the data *at a given point in time*. This proviso is important: just because something is right *now* does not mean it will always be right! More and better data may be uncovered which points to other conclusions; more efficient or creative theories may be put forward; a new and unexpected discovery may shake up the whole field – although this is not a common occurrence. As you progress as an education student, therefore, it is important that you learn to explore alternative viewpoints, approaching all research with a critical eye.

CROSS REFERENCE

Chapter 3, Becoming a member of your academic and professional community, Teaching, research and knowledge, Advanced skills, Research reports

CROSS REFERENCE

Chapter 3, Becoming a member of your academic and professional community, Teaching, research and knowledge

Critical thinking in education

Critical thinking is an important aspect of a teacher's professional practice. Ghaye and Ghaye (1998, p 9) maintained that:

> Teaching is value-laden practice. Values help teachers to make decisions on how to proceed. Evidence helps teachers make wise and principled decisions. Confident and competent teaching requires teachers to reflect systematically and rigorously on evidence derived from practice. Reflective teaching and learning then is evidence-based.

CROSS
REFERENCE

Chapter 3,
Becoming
a member
of your
academic and
professional
community,
Reflective
practice

Ghaye and Ghaye go on to suggest five types of reflections-on-practice:

- descriptive reflection-on-practice, which is personal and retrospective;
- perceptive reflection-on-practice, which links teaching to feelings;
- receptive reflection-on-practice, which relates your views to others' views;
- interactive reflection-on-practice, which links learning to future action;
- critical reflection-on-practice, which places individual teaching within a 'broader' system.

(Ghaye and Ghaye, 1998, p 9)

In considering reflection-on-practice, it is worth asking yourself who will benefit from your reflection and what the impact might be. For example, at the end of a lesson you might consider how your planning, use of resources, teaching and attitude to subject matter affected pupils' progress. You might then consider what you could do differently in your next lesson to improve pupils' progress. As Sellars (2017) concludes:

> It is this professional reflection, planning and commitment that allows you to support students' learning outcomes productively in your classroom and to promote the positive professional relationships that have the potential to engage and motivate even the most reluctant learners and begin your professional career as a teacher of quality.

(Sellars, 2017, p 287)

Applying and developing your critical thinking skills

As a trainee teacher, it is important to take a critical approach to every aspect of your studies and practice. You should be critical in the way you approach tasks, use sources of information, and present your work and ideas, both in your study activities, and in written, oral and practical assessments.

Approaching learning resources critically

As a university student, you will find information and ideas in many sources, the main ones being lectures, textbooks and academic journals. Lectures are delivered by people who are authorities in the field. Textbooks and academic journals are trusted because they are peer reviewed. Other sources, such as the media, websites, blogs, videos and podcasts may also be useful in certain contexts, but these should be used with extreme care, as it is harder to assess their credibility.

Taking a critical approach to source use means taking time to assess the relevance, credibility and authority of each particular source. Below are some questions which will help you to do this:

- Who wrote or created it? If it was a 'corporate' author (an organisation rather than a person writing the source), is that organisation credible?

- Are the authors considered to be an authority in the field?
- Do they have a relevant professional affiliation?
- Are they cited by scholars in other books and articles?
- What is the publication date?
- Is it the latest edition of a book?
- Are there more recent sources which may advance or question the content?
- Who is the intended reader or listener?
- What is the scope of the work?
- Is it published by an educational publisher or in a reputable academic journal?

Task

Look at the following sources and decide if they are credible sources for education students:

1) *Cambridge Journal of Education*
2) *British Journal of Educational Studies*
3) *British Educational Research Journal*
4) *Early Education Journal*
5) *Education 3–13*
6) *Teach Primary*
7) *Times Educational Supplement*
8) Ofsted (2011) *How Young Learners Master Maths: Ofsted Report on Best Practice in Early Arithmetic*. London: Crown.

Discussion

(1), (2), (3), (4) and (5) are international peer-reviewed journals publishing high-quality original research. This means that all articles submitted to them are looked at in detail by other academics who assess the credibility of the research described and the presentation of data and the authors' conclusions. They may then recommend that an article is accepted, revised or rejected. Sometimes articles in such journals are accompanied or followed by articles from other academics who contest the views of the authors.

Teach Primary (6) includes contributions from teachers, academics and other educators on a range of issues. Articles are subject to editing and revision, but are not generally based on original research, although they may describe innovative practice and its impact. The magazine also provides lesson ideas, reviews of resources and news of events. It is an excellent resource for primary teachers, but should be cited sparingly in academic essays.

The Times Educational Supplement (TES) (7) is an important source of information on a range of educational issues, including commentaries on government initiatives, international practice and innovative practice in schools. It also produces reports which summarise research and may lead readers to seek out the journals in which it is published. Although it can be an excellent starting point for finding out about research, it would be advisable to cite the original sources in journals in academic essays.

Ofsted reports (8) are generally summaries of the findings of inspectors in several inspections over a period of time. They provide invaluable insights into practice in schools nationwide and can be a useful source for academic essays, although it would be wise to look at academic sources in peer-reviewed journals for different perspectives.

Top tips

CROSS
REFERENCE

Chapter 5,
Academic
resources:
technology
and the library,
The university
library,
Knowing
what's
out there

Choosing the right source

Academic books include textbooks, edited collections, monographs (in-depth analyses of a subject), and reference works such as medical dictionaries. **Textbooks** (some of which are edited collections of chapters by different authors) are a good source of information and facts, and they are also useful in that they can provide an overview of the discipline (eg mathematics) or topic (eg calculus). They often summarise the way knowledge has developed in a certain area of education, sketching out the background and presenting the arguments that have been advanced along the way.

Journal articles often present a particular argument, usually through the reporting of a piece of research, with conclusions based on the results of that research. These journal articles will refer to other studies in order to provide a context for the current work. Some journal articles are 'review' articles, whose aim is to compare and contrast all the main studies that have been carried out in a particular area so as to identify any general tendencies or issues. Some journal articles are opinion pieces, but these are less common.

Active reading

Reading firstly requires you to actively engage any prior knowledge you have on a topic. This entails reflecting on what you already know or believe, and then looking out for particular things as you read. You need to be ready to notice anything interesting or important. Begin by asking yourself two questions:

- Why are you reading?
- What do you expect/hope to find out?

Looking at the items in Table 4.1 may help you determine to what extent the source will provide answers to your questions.

Table 4.1: Understanding the gist of books and articles

BOOK	JOURNAL ARTICLE
Title	Title
Blurb on the back cover	Abstract
Information about the author(s) (so you can check their credibility)	Information about the author(s) (so you can check their credibility)
Contents page	Headings and sub-headings
Introduction	Introduction
Chapter aims or learning outcomes listed at the start of each chapter (as in this book)	Figures and Tables (which visually summarise the evidence)
Conclusion	Discussion/Conclusion
Index	

Once you have identified a source as potentially useful, the next step in active reading usually involves taking notes or highlighting important information. However you do this, you should be systematic in your approach, as this can save time and effort later on.

Synthesis of information and ideas

At the beginning of your undergraduate studies, you will be required to demonstrate your *understanding* of dominant theories or important studies. As you progress, you will be expected to show an increasing awareness of alternative viewpoints on a topic and of the importance of evidence in evaluating them. As you do this, you need to find ways of categorising and **synthesising** information and ideas. For example, if you are reading to find out about the relative merits of different approaches to teaching reading, it might be useful if you create a table or database like the one below.

Table 4.2: Developing children's reading at Key Stage 2

(Adapted from Higgins et al (2017))

SUPPORT PUPILS TO DEVELOP A FLUENT READING STYLE	TEACH READING COMPREHENSION STRATEGIES THROUGH MODELLING AND SUPPORTED PRACTICE
Summary of findings Fluent readers can read quickly, accurately and with appropriate stress and intonation. A fluent reading style supports comprehension because pupils' limited cognitive resources are freed from focusing on word recognition and can be redirected towards comprehending the text. This can be developed through: – **Guided oral reading instruction** – fluent reading of a text is modelled and pupils then read the same text aloud with appropriate feedback. – **Repeated reading** – pupils re-read a short and meaningul passage a set number of times or until they reach a suitable level of fluency.	**Summary of findings** Reading comprehension can be improved by teaching specific strategies that can be applied to both monitor and develop reading comprehension. These include: – prediction – questioning – clarifying – summarising – inference – activating prior knowledge These strategies should be described and modelled before pupils practise the strategies with feedback and gradually reduced support. Good text selection supports the teaching of reading comprehension strategies: too easy and pupils do not need to use the strategies, too hard and the strategies will not help.
Key sources Scarborough, HS (2001) Connecting Early Language and Literacy to Later Reading (Dis) Abilities: Evidence, Theory, and Practice. In Neuman, S and Dickinson, D (eds) *Handbook for Research in Early Literacy*. New York: Guilford Press, 97–110. Savage, R, Burgos, G, Wood, E and Piquette, N (2015) The Simple View of Reading as a Framework for National Literacy Initiatives: A Hierarchical Model of Pupil-Level and Classroom-Level Factors. *British Educational Research Journal*, 41(5), 820–44. Available at: http://dx.doi.org/10.1002/berj.3177(accessed 17 February 2018).	**Key sources** https://educationendowment foundation.org.uk/resources/teaching-learning-toolkit/reading-comprehension-strategies/ (accessed 17 February 2018). Oakhill, J, Cain, K and Elbro, C (2014) *Understanding and Teaching Reading Comprehension: A Handbook*. London: Routledge. http://etd.library.vanderbilt.edu/available/etd-06162010-100830/unrestricted/Davis_dissertation.pdf (accessed 17 February 2018).

SUPPORT PUPILS TO DEVELOP A FLUENT READING STYLE	TEACH READING COMPREHENSION STRATEGIES THROUGH MODELLING AND SUPPORTED PRACTICE
Torgerson, CJ, Brooks, G and Hall, J (2006) *A Systematic Review of the Research Literature on the Use of Phonics in the Teaching of Reading and Spelling.* London: Department for Education and Skills. Price-Mohr, R and Price, C (2016) Gender Differences in Early Reading Strategies: A Comparison of Synthetic Phonics Only With a Mixed Approach to Teaching Reading to 4–5 Year-Old Children. *Early Childhood Education Journal*, 1–8. Goswami, U (2008) Reading, Complexity and the Brain. *Literacy*, 42(2), 67–74. Swanson, H and O'Connor, R (2009) The Role of Working Memory and Fluency Practice on the Reading Comprehension of Students Who Are Dysfluent Readers. *Journal of Learning Disabilities*, 42(6), 548–75. National Reading Panel (US) (2000) *Teaching Children to Read: An Evidence-Based Assessment of the Scientific Research Literature on Reading and Its Implications for Reading Instruction.* Washington, DC: National Institute of Child Health and Human Development, National Institutes of Health. Therrien, W (2004) Fluency and Comprehension Gains as a Result of Repeated Reading. Remedial and Special Education, 25(4), 252–61.	National Reading Panel (2000) *Teaching Children to Read: An Evidence-Based Assessment of the Scientific Research Literature on Reading and Its Implications for Reading Instruction – Reports of the Subgroups.* Washington, DC: National Institute of Child Health and Human Development. Stuart, M and Stainthorp, R (2015) *Reading Development and Teaching.* London: Sage. https://educationendowmentfoundation.org.uk/resources/teaching-learning-toolkit/meta-cognition-and-self-regulation/ (accessed 17 February 2018). McKenna, MC and Stahl, KAD (2015) *Assessment for Reading Instruction.* 3rd ed. New York: Guilford Publications. https://educationendowmentfoundation.org.uk/resources/teaching-learning-toolkit/collaborative-learning/ (accessed 17 February 2018). Spörer, N, Brunstein, JC and Kieschke, ULF (2009) Improving Students' Reading Comprehension Skills: Effects of Strategy Instruction and Reciprocal Teaching. *Learning and Instruction*, 19(3), 272–86.
Evidence strength Very extensive Extensive **Moderate** Limited Very limited	**Evidence strength** **Very extensive** Extensive Moderate Limited Very limited

Table 4.2 sums up key findings and shows where the evidence for these come from and the strength of the evidence. This is based upon a meta-analysis, whereby researchers analyse a range of key research and draw conclusions based upon this.

As you gather information and ideas in this way, you should do so with a critical eye. Active, critical reading may involve:

- identifying developments in knowledge and thinking among scholars;
- comparing and contrasting ideas, theories and findings;
- identifying shared or contrasting views and the reasoning behind them;
- identifying, examining and evaluating evidence;
- comparing the scope of different studies;
- comparing the conclusions of different studies;
- discerning relationships and patterns, and things which do not seem to 'fit in' with everything else;
- relating ideas, theories and research to your existing knowledge and the current context, eg the essay question in hand.

Advanced skills

CROSS
REFERENCE

Academic
Writing and
Referencing,
Chapter 3,
Referring to
sources

Originality

Originality is part of critical thinking, which becomes more important as you advance in your studies, so it is important to understand what is meant by 'original' in academia. It is unusual to be original in the sense of spontaneously coming up with an entirely new idea in academia, but a new perspective on how things relate to each other is a valid example of original thought. This treatment of information and ideas is a type of '*knowledge **transformation**'*, as opposed to the simpler process of '*knowledge **telling**'* (Beireiter and Scardamalia, 1987). These concepts will be further explored in *Academic Writing and Referencing*, as the relationship between criticality, intelligent use of sources, and originality is examined.

Scrutinising research and arguments

A great deal of academic discourse is devoted to putting forward arguments. When reading or listening to these arguments, you need to isolate and identify the author's line of reasoning, and then evaluate it according to clear criteria.

- Is the argument clearly articulated, for example in the introduction to a book or article? Is this reflected in the content of the book or article?
- Is the argument developed in a logical way? Is it based on sound reasoning? Does each stage of the argument follow on logically from the next? Does everything *make sense*?

- Is there sufficient evidence to support the argument? Is it credible and convincing? Does it lead naturally to the conclusion, or could other valid conclusions be drawn?
- Have alternative viewpoints and possibilities been explored?

Adopting a critical approach means looking out for anything which might weaken the argument you are listening to or reading. There are certain terms which may help you to critique an argument (some of which are sometimes used by lecturers when they critique (mark) assessments).

Task

Match the terms on the left with the correct definition on the right. (The first one has been done as an example.)

Premise	A reason for doing something which is often not directly declared
Assumption	Not supported by facts
Agenda	Ideas on which subsequent ideas or actions are based
Anecdotal	Something which is accepted as true without question or proof
Bias	The action of supporting or opposing someone or something in an unfair way, allowing personal opinion to influence your judgement
Subjective	Based on personal experience rather than research
Unsubstantiated	Based on personal beliefs and feelings, rather than on facts

Reflection

1) Look at the claims below and decide if there is anything which weakens them. For example:

- Are there any false premises?
- Is there any bias?
- Is the argument subjective?
- Is the argument unbalanced?
- Could the writer/speaker have an agenda?
- Is the data reliable?
- Is there is any evidence which is purely anecdotal?

- Are assertions, appeals etc based on emotional appeal or personal anecdote rather than logical reasoning?
- Are there are any assumptions, overgeneralisations or unsubstantiated claims?
- Is there any inconsistency or ambiguity?
- Is there any flawed reasoning?

a) Ten years ago, 20 per cent of students got the top grade in their exam. Now, 40 per cent do. This proves that exams are getting easier.

b) Children from poor families do less well at school because their parents don't read to them at home.

c) Boys don't do as well as girls in reading because they prefer playing computer games to reading.

d) Children from Chinese backgrounds always work hard in school. I had a girl in my last class and she was really conscientious.

e) Everyone I've spoken to agrees that children don't need to learn grammatical terms because they can still read and write without knowing them.

f) The best way to teach early reading is to adopt a systematic synthetic phonics programme.

g) When I was at school teachers used to hit us if we were naughty and it never did me any harm.

2) Identify some examples of problematic language usage, for example 'proves' in a).

If an argument or theory is reported in a journal article, conference paper or an academic textbook, there are particular questions you should bear in mind as you read:

- Are the writers qualified to carry out the research? Are they authorities on the subject? What is their professional role? Do they have any vested interests?
- What are the objectives of the study? Are they clearly articulated?
- What is the problem or 'gap' in the knowledge that the study addresses?
- What is the hypothesis or research question behind the study?
- Do the writers provide sufficient context and lay the ground for their research question?
- Is the relevant literature reviewed?
- Is the methodology sound? Could it be reproduced by other scholars?
- Are the authors reporting on their own research or summarising other people's research?
- Are the interpretations of the results credible?
- Have the implications of the study for educational practice been correctly identified?
- Have the limitations of the study been acknowledged?
- Has the study advanced knowledge in the field of education?

Task

> **Look at the following extract from the introduction to a published chapter (Higgins, S in Waugh and Neaum, 2013) and see how many of the above questions you can answer. (You would need to access the full chapter to answer *all* the questions.)**

Why do we need research?

Imagine going to see your local doctor and hearing her (or him) say, 'Oh I don't keep up to date with research. I just use the things that I know work for my patients. I learned what I know on the job, so I'm not really interested in how research can help me or my patients'. Would you be impressed? Of course, medical research and educational research are different, but we can still learn valuable lessons from what research tells us will help make us more effective teachers, which will keep us up to date with evidence as it develops, and which will help keep us effective and fresh as teachers through trying out and evaluating new ideas.

International comparisons

There are a number of large-scale international comparisons of educational performance. The oldest is the Trends in International Mathematics and Science Study (TIMSS), which was first administered in 1995 by the International Association for the Evaluation of Educational Achievement (IEA) to allow the countries involved to compare their pupils' educational attainment in mathematics and science. The IEA also manages the Progress in International Reading Literacy Study (PIRLS), which assesses 9–10-year-olds in reading and literacy (see below). The Programme for International Student Assessment (PISA) is another international study, undertaken by the Organisation for Economic Co-operation and Development (OECD), of 15-year-old school pupils' attainment in mathematics, science and reading. It was first administered in 2000 and then repeated every three years. These studies can help us to understand how our children are learning compared with progress in other countries. They also can shed light on other debates, such as the age that children start school, and on the teaching of the subjects that are assessed, including literacy. The tests and the design of the sampling of pupils aim to make the fairest comparisons possible, given differences in language and culture.

Progress in International Reading Literacy Study (PIRLS) 2011

The Progress in International Reading Literacy Study (PIRLS) is an international study of reading. It is conducted by the International Association for the Evaluation of Educational Achievement (IEA). It has measured trends in the reading and literacy achievement of 9–10 year-olds every five years since 2001. It also collects information about reading and literacy policies, teaching practices in schools and home experiences. In 2006 PIRLS tested over 215,000 pupils aged 9–10 years, from 45 countries.

In 2011, the results showed that only five out of the 45 countries involved performed significantly better than England. These countries were Hong Kong, the Russian Federation, Singapore, Finland and Northern Ireland.

England's performance improved between 2006 and 2011. Only the United States and Chinese Taipei showed greater improvement in this period.

Pupils in England had a wider spread of attainment than the top performing countries. The highest attaining pupils in England were similar to those in Singapore and higher than the best readers in the three top performing countries (Hong Kong, the Russian Federation and Finland). However, low attaining pupils in England scored less well than the low attaining pupils in other countries.

This indicates that overall progress in reading at primary school in England and Northern Ireland is good compared with other countries around the world (Scotland did not take part in PIRLS). It also suggests that although the highest attaining pupils in England do as well as the best countries in the world for reading, we are not as good as these countries in supporting the reading achievement of our lower attaining pupils. England had one of the largest proportions of pupils reaching the Advanced International Benchmark (18 per cent). However, the proportion of pupils in England who did not reach the Low International Benchmark (5 per cent) is similar to the proportion that do not achieve level 3 or above in National Curriculum tests of reading in England at the end of primary school. Overall this international evidence therefore suggests that this is an area where we could improve our overall performance, and at the same time provide a more equitable education system for our children. In other countries the gap between the highest and lowest attaining pupils does not widen as much as it does in England.

Gender and attainment in literacy

International comparisons can provide information about more than overall national performance or the spread of scores however. We worry a lot in the UK about the underperformance of boys and the difficulties that boys seem to have in literacy and in particular early reading and writing, but what is the evidence for this from PIRLS? It is certainly true that girls performed significantly better than boys in PIRLS in England, but this is true for almost all other participating countries, with scores for girls on average about 3 per cent better than boys. So, girls all over the world, on average, do a little bit better on tests of literacy at age 10. It is also true that the difference between the attainment of boys and girls is a little bit bigger in England than in most other countries, and this has stayed about the same in all three PIRLS surveys. So the problem is an international one, and we do a little less well than other countries at solving it. The difference between the UK and the average of the other countries is just less than 1 per cent however. So although there is a difference, and that difference hasn't really changed since 2001, it is a very small difference. It is also true to say that the difference between boys and girls is not as great as the 'gap' between low attaining and high attaining pupils' results in PIRLS. We have 5 per cent of our pupils who don't even reach the low benchmark, whereas 99 per cent of the pupils in Hong Kong, and 98 per cent of the pupils in the Russian Federation, Sweden and the United States do.

Demonstrating criticality in your academic work

So far, you have focused on how to think critically. However, it is not only important to *think* critically; you must know how to *demonstrate* your critical thinking in all your academic work, both through the content, and with careful use of language.

Discussion versus description

To demonstrate criticality in your work, there must be a high level of **discussion** throughout. To do this successfully, it is necessary to understand the difference between *description* and *discussion*, and to recognise these things in your reading, and in your own work.

Task

1) Look back at the introduction section of the article extract in the previous task and identify which parts of the text are:
   - description;
   - discussion.
2) Which words and phrases helped you to recognise these two things?

As you write, or present work orally, you will usually move from description to discussion. As you progress through your undergraduate studies, you will be expected to engage in increasingly complex levels of discussion.

Increasing complexity

Description

- Presenting facts.

Discussion

- Demonstrating understanding of a topic through analysis and evaluation.
- Demonstrating understanding of debates and alternate viewpoints, and their associated evidence.
- Weighing up the evidence for one side or another.
- Revealing the implications of different aspects of your analysis and evaluation for your overall argument.
- Guiding the reader or listener through the process by which you arrived at your conclusions.

Figure 4.2: Levels of complexity in discussion

CROSS REFERENCE

Academic Writing and Referencing

Stance

While it is important to include the views of scholars and authorities in your work, this must be as part of the wider primary objective, which is to say what *you* think. You need to feel able to let your own voice emerge. Your opinion, supported by research and evidence, is known as your **stance**, ie your position on the topic;

what you believe, with good reason, to be true or correct. This becomes more important as you advance in your studies.

Adopting and maintaining a stance requires confidence. You need to feel secure in your understanding of the issues and your ability to persuade. There is no easy route to attaining this kind of confidence; it is something you will build over time and with experience. You may find that your stance is different from that of your lecturer. This is fine, as long as you present a clear rationale and evidence to support your view.

Top tips

Developing your stance

CROSS REFERENCE

Chapter 2, *Studying for your Education Degree*, Working independently, working in teams

1) Test your understanding, ideas and opinions through discussion in study groups. Arrange to get together informally with other students to discuss important topics. This type of collaboration is a valid part of academic life: this is what your lecturers do when they network at conferences. Of course, you must be careful that it doesn't spill over into 'collusion' (ie working together in order to deceive), which counts as academic malpractice.

2) Start writing! Getting words down on paper is one of the best ways to clarify your own thinking. As you struggle with meaning and expression, you may reveal misunderstandings and gaps in your knowledge, and expose vague ideas and ambiguities. You can then go back to your lecture notes, books and articles, or talk to lecturers and fellow students, and try to clear things up. When you return to the page, you will hopefully be able to improve the content and expression to reflect your new-found understanding, and thus be more confident in your stance!

Argument

CROSS REFERENCE

Academic Writing and Referencing, Chapter 1, Academic writing: text, process and criticality, The writing process

Taking a stance entails constructing an **argument** that will convince the reader or listener. As you do this, you must draw together support for your position, tying it into your own carefully constructed line of reasoning. This necessitates using information, ideas, arguments and evidence from the literature. As you are using these things to support your account or argument, it is very important that they are clearly and accurately explained.

You will need to demonstrate that you have approached your sources critically: that you have analysed, interpreted and evaluated the validity and credibility of the facts, ideas and opinions that you encounter; that you have carefully examined the reasoning behind claims, and the explanations, evidence and examples put forward in support of them.

Objectivity

It is important to demonstrate **objectivity** in your evaluation of the work of others. This involves being clear that your opinions have been formed on the basis of fact and evidence, rather than just personal feeling. You must show that you are not unduly biased in favour of a particular viewpoint or interpretation and that you are not being selective about the evidence you consider. You need to convey what you believe and provide justification for it. One way of doing this is to reference clearly, as this allows you to be transparent about what is influencing your opinion.

Persuasiveness

The aim of much academic writing is to persuade the reader through the quality of your argument. You will also help persuade the reader if there is a 'persuasive structure' to your argument. For example, laying the groundwork before you make a claim will make the claim stronger, because the reader or listener can see the basis for your argument; likewise, maintaining a strong thread of argument throughout your text will make your argument more coherent and therefore more convincing. Also, a calm, objective style is more convincing than an impassioned appeal, as it shows confidence in the ability of the facts to speak for themselves.

CROSS REFERENCE

Academic Writing and Referencing, Chapter 2, Coherence in texts and arguments

Top tips

Acknowledge complexity

Taking a stance is not the same as being stubborn! Most academic topics are complex, with no easy answers. Therefore, your stance should be nuanced. Analysing issues from multiple perspectives, and acknowledging strengths, weaknesses and grey areas will strengthen, not weaken your argument, as you are protecting it from attack for being too simplistic. In fact, it may well be that you find, after reviewing all the evidence, that there is not enough convincing support for one particular viewpoint and that further research is needed; many systematic literature reviews in reputable journals reach this very conclusion!

Case studies

Explain the critical thinking process that the teachers in the situations below would need to go through. You may wish to refer back to Figure 4.1 and reflect on the qualities they would need to demonstrate.

1) A parent of a Year 5 pupil comes to see her teacher to say that she feels her daughter is more able than other children on her table and should be moved to sit and work with a higher-ability group.

2) A Year 3 class includes a child, Jack, whom the teacher feels is on the autism spectrum. However, the child's parents do not wish to have him assessed and so, in the absence of a statement of need, no additional support can be provided for the child. The teacher has one teaching assistant assigned to her class to work with different children as and when necessary. The teacher would like to ask her to work more with Jack and would also like the parents to agree to Jack being assessed by experts in autism.

3) A trainee teacher sees an experienced teacher manhandling a badly behaved child in a way she feels is unnecessarily rough. She cannot decide whether to speak to the teacher, the headteacher or to ignore what she has seen and not mention it to anyone.

Summary

This chapter has introduced the concept of criticality and examined its role in academic life and teaching practice. It has suggested ways of approaching learning and sources in a critical way. It has provided strategies for critical reading and provided a framework for approaching academic journal articles. It has identified strategies for presenting your ideas critically in assessments.

References

Beireiter, C and Scardamalia, M (1987) *The Psychology of Written Composition*. Hillsdale, NJ: Lawrence Erlbaum Associates.

Chambers 21st Century Dictionary (1999) Edinburgh: Chambers Harrap Publishers Ltd.

Ghaye, A and Ghaye, K (1998) *Teaching and Learning through Critical Reflective Practice*. London: David Fulton.

Higgins, S (2013) What Can We Learn from Research? In Waugh, D and Neaum, S (eds) *Beyond Early Reading*. Northwich: Critical Publishing.

Higgins, S, Henderson, P, Martell, T, Sharples, J and Waugh, D (2017) *Improving Literacy in Key Stage 2: Guidance Report*. London: EEF. Available at: https://educationendowmentfoundation.org.uk/evidence/school-themes/literacy/ (accessed 17 February 2018).

Merriam-Webster Dictionary [online]. Available at: www.merriam-webster.com (accessed 16 February 2018).

Oxford Living Dictionaries: English [online]. Available at: https://en.oxforddictionaries.com/ (accessed 16 February 2018).

Sellars, M (2017) *Reflective Practice for Teachers*. 2nd ed. London: Sage.

Chapter 5
Academic resources: technology and the library

Learning outcomes

After reading this chapter you will:

- have gained an understanding of technology and the scope of the technological resources available to you at university;

- be able to access a range of computer hardware and software with confidence;

- appreciate the value and the limitations of the internet;

- understand the standards and regulations which govern the use of technology in universities;

- be prepared to make effective use of the university library;

- be able to carry out a basic literature search.

CROSS REFERENCE

Chapter 1, Studying education in higher education

The aim of this chapter is to provide you with knowledge and strategies which will enable you to make full use of the resources available to you at university. It will help you understand how technology and the university library can help you develop your research and communication skills, and generally enhance your educational studies.

For a discussion of the role of e-learning methods and tools such as blended learning and Virtual Learning Environments (VLEs), see Chapter 1.

Understanding technology and developing good computer skills

In its strictest sense, 'technology' is the application of science to practical, real-world situations; it is *applied* science. Since learning is inextricably linked to *information*, educators are primarily concerned with **information technology (IT)**, or **information and communication technology (ICT)**.

It is useful to divide technology into two components: **hardware** and **software**.

Hardware

Hardware is the physical equipment that you can touch. It includes:

- computers, including laptops and tablets;

- phones, including landlines, mobiles and smartphones;

- media recorders such as cameras and camcorders;
- media players such as MP3, CD and DVD players;
- portable storage devices known as pen drives, USB memory sticks etc;
- gaming consoles such as Wii, Nintendo DS, Xbox and PlayStation.

Reflection

1) How might the different types of hardware be of use to you in your university studies and in teaching practice?

2) What issues or problems may accompany their use?

Discussion of hardware uses at university

Compare your ideas from the reflection with those in Table 5.1.

Table 5.1: Types of hardware

HARDWARE	SOME USES	SOME ISSUES AND PROBLEMS
Computers	Main research and communication tool (discussed in detail later in the next section); laptops and tablets useful for note-taking in lectures	Information on the internet must be treated with caution; overuse may lead to conditions such as repetitive strain injury (RSI)
Phones	Contacting students and lecturers; photographing the screen during lectures	Need to be aware of 'mobile phone etiquette' such as making sure phones are silenced in lectures (not turned off – there may be legitimate use of a phone in a lecture, accessing a dictionary for example); may need permission for some photos
Media recorders and players	Recording and playing back recorded material such as lectures and interviews	Make sure you have permission to record things
Portable storage devices	Backing up files and moving files between devices	Small pen drives are easy to misplace – many are left behind in university computer drives; security issues – computer viruses are easily transferred with these

HARDWARE	SOME USES	SOME ISSUES AND PROBLEMS
Gaming consoles	Some have suggested educational uses, but they are perhaps mostly useful for helping some people to switch off and relax	Make sure they don't distract you from study or disrupt your sleep patterns

Computers in particular are now an essential part of studying. They are invaluable tools for word processing assignments, creating presentation slides, searching for information, carrying out statistical analysis, and communicating with others.

Most universities are extremely well resourced when it comes to computers, with 'clusters' of computers set up throughout their campuses. Almost all the computers in a university are 'networked' (joined to one another), and to access them you will need a **username** and **password**. Details of how to obtain these will be provided when you commence your programme of study.

Software

Software is what runs on the hardware to enable you to process the information you are interested in. With the advent of smartphones, tablets and other portable devices, software has come to be known as **apps** (from 'software applications').

It will benefit your studies if you can develop an understanding of what software is available, and how you can access and use it.

Office suites

Office suites are integrated software packages containing a number of different programs that are useful in an office, business or educational environment. As a minimum, they include word processing, presentation and spreadsheet software, but many other components are available to suit individual needs. The most well-known office suites are **Microsoft Office** and **OpenOffice**. Microsoft Office is a commercial program which you normally have to pay for, but free access is almost always provided by universities for registered students. OpenOffice is 'open source', meaning that it is freely available; it is also compatible with Microsoft Office, which means users can work across systems easily. The software in these suites resides on individual computers or, in large organisations such as universities, on a server which manages access to centralised resources and services in the network. **Google Docs** and Apple's **iWork** are slightly different types of office suite in that their software sits in the cloud on the internet rather than on a computer or server; cloud technology is further discussed later in the chapter.

As a university student, you will probably receive a free account such as **Office 365** for the duration of your studies. This will give you access to software, including email.

The components of an office suite that are likely to be most useful to you in your studies are:

CROSS
REFERENCE

Advanced
skills,
Advanced
software

- word processing software;
- presentation software;
- spreadsheet software;
- communication software.

You may also use software to help you analyse data or to help you reference, as discussed later in the chapter.

Word processing

Word processing packages turn your computer into a sophisticated typewriter. The most well known is **Microsoft Word**. Word processing offers huge advantages over hand-writing and old-fashioned typewriting: documents can be easily edited; many different fonts are available; pictures and diagrams can be easily inserted into documents; links to other documents can be included via **hyperlinks** (highlighted words or images which you can click on); tools are available to help you format documents professionally.

CROSS
REFERENCE

Academic
Writing and
Referencing,
Chapter 5,
Preparing
your work for
submission

Top tips

Formatting

Try not to think of formatting as something merely 'cosmetic', there just to make the page look nice. Clear presentation will make your work instantly more professional. What's more, clear and consistent formatting will contribute to the **coherence** of the text. Carefully distinguished headings and sub-headings, together with clearly set out paragraphs and sections, will help the reader move smoothly through the text. A well-chosen font (Times New Roman or Arial) and font size (usually 12pt) will also positively affect the reader's experience, as will the use of 1.5 or double line spacing. Last but not least, don't forget page numbers. (Pity the poor lecturer shuffling papers on the train to work!)

Word processing software has many user-friendly tools, available on the tool bar as icons or in drop-down menus. These include 'cut' and 'paste', which allows you to move text around easily, and the 'undo' command, which allows you to reverse one or several actions.

Top tips

Keyboard shortcuts

If you use the **Microsoft Windows** operating system, as the majority of students do, there are a number of keyboard shortcuts which will save you time and effort (ctrl = control, the key in the bottom left-hand corner of your keyboard):

ctrl O = open file

ctrl S = save file

ctrl P = print file

ctrl A = select all the text in a document

ctrl C = copy selected text or item

ctrl X = cut selected text or item

ctrl V = paste selected text or item

ctrl Z = undo previous action

ctrl B = make selected text **bold**

ctrl I = make selected text *italic*

ctrl U = <u>underline</u> selected text

Apple Mac shortcuts can be found here:

https://support.apple.com/en-gb/HT201236

Presentations

The most well-known presentation software is **Microsoft PowerPoint**, but **Prezi** is also increasingly popular. With both of these, a series of slides is created which form the basis of a presentation, and these can be formatted by choosing a suitable slide design, font etc. There is also the possibility of creating or uploading pictures, diagrams etc. These slides can be very simple, or layers of complexity can be added through the use of the **transition** (movement between slides) and **animation** (movement within slides) tools. With PowerPoint, you move through the slides chronologically during your presentation; with Prezi, you pan between topics, zooming in on detail or zooming out to reveal the wider context.

It is important to make your slides readable for everyone in the audience, and to make your presentation as inclusive as possible. This entails making provision, where you can, for audience members who may have a particular condition, such as visual impairment, or a specific learning difficulty, such as dyslexia.

Top tips

Presentation slides

- Choose a font size that's visible at the back of the room (24pt is usually the lower limit, but it depends on other factors – room, size of screen etc).
- Be wary of using **bold**, *italics*, <u>underlining</u> or CAPITALISATION to convey subtleties of meaning, as these are hard to read on screen, particularly for anyone who is dyslexic.
- Don't make the slides too cluttered with text or images.
- Make sure diagrams and labels are clearly visible.
- Avoid decorative background images that may obscure the text.
- Make sure there is a clear colour contrast between background and text (and remember that just because it's clear on your computer at home, it doesn't mean it necessarily will be on a classroom screen with different resolution and lighting conditions – always check *in situ*).

CROSS
REFERENCE

Communication Skills, Chapter 1, Academic presentations and public speaking

- Avoid using red and green together, as people who have a colour vision deficiency (the formal name for 'colour blindness') cannot distinguish between them.
- Moving images or flashing effects can be distracting or even irritating – they may also be dangerous for people with epilepsy or light-sensitivity.
- If you use the animation **appear** function, plan how to synchronise the appearance of each bullet point with a segment of your speech – there's no point using the appear function if you introduce all the bullet points at once.

See *Communication Skills* for more tips on creating and delivering presentations.

Top tips

Presentation technology: less is more?

There is no doubt that PowerPoint and Prezi are very visual tools with an effective 'story telling' function which can genuinely help you convey information and ideas. What's more, clever use of diagrams, transitions and animations can truly enhance your presentation: for example, an audience could be guided through a teaching sequence for writing, which is gradually revealed using the 'appear' function. The diagram below could be presented and explained in three separate stages (1; +2; +3), allowing the audience to process one piece of information before moving on to the next:

Figure 5.1: A possible teaching sequence for writing

However, any 'special effects' should be integral to the main aim of the presentation, which should always be to convey information and ideas in the clearest possible way to the audience. Too many 'showy' animations can be a distraction.

Ultimately, presentation software is an **organisational tool**, and complex ideas almost always benefit from a **simple organisational structure** and **clear and consistent formatting**.

Spreadsheets

Spreadsheet software is extremely useful for work which requires mathematical or financial calculations. The most well known is **Microsoft Excel**. While you won't use spreadsheet software as much as word processing and presentation software in your studies, spreadsheets have a range of uses in education. For example, they can be used to show and analyse information about pupil performance in relation to factors such as free school meals, ethnicity and gender.

Top tips

Working smart

As a student, it won't be long before you have created a number of different files, be they word processing documents, presentations or spreadsheets, and it is extremely important that you know where these are and that you don't somehow lose or inadvertently delete them.

1) Always make sure you **save**, and ideally, **back up** your work. There are many ways to save work, including:

   - your university's networked drive;

   - a USB memory stick;

   - cloud services such as **Dropbox**, **Google Docs**, **Apple iCloud** and **OneDrive**.

   The most secure of these is your university's networked drive, as it can only be accessed using your university login and password, and, crucially, it is backed up frequently by the university, so it is extremely unlikely that you will lose your work. In addition, as it is networked, you can access this drive anywhere in the world as long as you have an internet connection. For these reasons, this is the best way to save your work, particularly anything which is important.

   You may also choose to use USB memory sticks and cloud services, but be aware of the limitations of these. As mentioned earlier, USB sticks are easy to lose and can transmit viruses. Cloud services may not necessarily be backed up and, more importantly, they may not meet UK or university data protection requirements.

2) Make sure you organise your work in a systematic way. It is a good idea to create folders to save your work according to topic; otherwise, your drive will soon become unwieldy and untidy. Experiment with organisational systems until you find something that works for you. Choose file names which are as short and simple as possible, but which easily identify the content of a file and distinguish it from others. Some people add the date to the file name (eg literacydeveptessay-02feb16.doc), which is useful if you want to keep and go back to an earlier version of your work – to restore something you deleted, for example.

Communication software

You can use computers to communicate in a variety of ways. These include: email, messaging and **Skype/FaceTime**, all of which require an internet connection. There is a variety of email software, including the cloud-based **Microsoft Outlook**, which is included in Office 365, and web-based email services such as Google's **Gmail**.

Top tips

Your university email address

Your university will provide you with a university email, and even though you may well have one or more other email accounts, you should always use your university email to communicate with staff and other students and for all university business. As you will no doubt be aware, there is a huge amount of junk email, or 'spam' about. With a view to managing spam, universities have filtering systems, and this may affect emails from web-based accounts, especially if the address contains dubious words! You should check your university account regularly as this is how the university will contact you. This is also where VLE updates and announcements will automatically be sent.

Messaging services can be synchronous or asynchronous: synchronous means that all the participants in the 'chat' can communicate at the same time; asynchronous means that each piece of text has to be posted somewhere, ie to a relevant discussion board or forum, and participants have to wait for responses.

The most well-known synchronous service is instant messaging – you may be familiar with examples such as **WhatsApp**. Instant messaging 'chat' can be restricted to those you know or invite, or it can take place with lesser-known acquaintances or even strangers in what are known as 'chat rooms'. This software is especially useful for communicating over long distances, and it now often includes audio and video functions.

Asynchronous messaging is commonly conducted in universities through **discussion boards**, which are usually part of your VLE. Unlike with synchronous messaging, the messages you post on discussion boards will usually be archived, so there will be a permanent record. It is therefore worth taking a little longer to consider the tone and content of your posts.

CROSS
REFERENCE

Communication Skills, Chapter 4, Networking

Skype provides all the basics of instant messaging plus phone use. Some members of staff at university may choose to communicate with you using Skype, especially if they are working away from the university for some reason.

Advanced skills

Advanced software

Your university library will probably provide information and training on a number of more specialised software applications.

1) Third-year undergraduates and postgraduates will probably need technical help in analysing their data. Those undertaking **quantitative** research (research including 'quantities', ie numbers) may need to make use of specialised **statistical software**. The most well-known of these are **SPSS** and **Stata**. Those undertaking **qualitative** research (research concerned with 'qualities', ie experiences, feelings, perceptions etc) might use software like **Nvivo** to help them manage and analyse their data.

2) As you begin to write longer, fully-referenced essays and dissertations, you may choose to employ referencing management software such as **Endnote**, **Mendeley**, **Zotero** and **Papyrus**.

The internet

CROSS REFERENCE

Academic Writing and Referencing, Chapter 3, Referring to sources

The internet is the most powerful information and communication tool in existence, and it has transformed all our lives. You will no doubt be aware of both its potential and its challenges in modern society.

Reflection

Pros and cons of the internet

Consider some of the positive and negative aspects of the internet in each of the following areas (which are discussed in more detail in the rest of this section):

1) information retrieval, in particular on topics related to education issues;

2) storing data and files online;

3) social media;

4) security.

The internet is a vast global collection of computers. The computers in your university will be connected to the internet and you will probably have a **broadband** connection at home. The most important part of the internet is the **World Wide Web**, or 'the **Web**', containing text, images, videos etc, and usually **hypertext** (links to other web pages). Web pages have a **URL** (Uniform Resource Locator) address beginning with 'www.'. For example, the URL of the Department for Education is www.gov. uk/government/organisations/department-for-education. Different websites have different 'domain names' (at the end of the address) depending on their status, eg:

- .com = company;
- .org.uk = UK charities;
- .gov.uk = official UK government sites;
- .ac.uk = UK universities.

Below are some websites you may find useful during your educational studies:

Table 5.2: Useful education websites

ORGANISATION	BRIEF DETAILS	WEB ADDRESS
GENERAL WEBSITES		
Department for Education	Information about all aspects of education in England and Wales	www.gov.uk/government/organisations/department-for-education (accessed 17 February 2018)
Department of Education of Northern Ireland	Information about all aspects of education in Northern Ireland	www.education-ni.gov.uk/ (accessed 17 February 2018)
GENERAL EDUCATION WEBSITES		
The Education Website	Information about all the various tests and exams currently in operation in the British education system	www.theeducationwebsite.co.uk/index.php?page=tests exams (accessed 17 February 2018)
WEBSITES PROVIDING RESEARCH INFORMATION		
National Foundation for Educational Research	Invaluable site for gaining access to key research and literature reviews	www.nfer.ac.uk/ (accessed 17 February 2018)
Education Endowment Foundation	Provides a range of resources, including summaries of key educational research	https://educationendowmentfoundation.org.uk/ (accessed 17 February 2018)
Times Educational Supplement (jobs	Provides details of education jobs in Britain and abroad	www.tes.com/jobs/ (accessed 17 February 2018)
PROFESSIONAL BODIES AND TEACHER UNIONS		
National Education Union	Largest teaching union in UK	www.teachers.org.uk/ (accessed 17 February 2018)
NASUWT	Large teachers' union in UK	www.nasuwt.org.uk/ (accessed 17 February 2018)
RESOURCES FOR TEACHING AND LEARNING		
Teachit Primary	Community of teachers contributing resources, discussing ideas and finding inspiration; membership gives access to free resources	www.teachitprimary.co.uk/ (accessed 17 February 2018)

| The Literacy Shed | Packed with ideas and resources, including images and videos to use in lessons | www.literacyshed.com/home.html (accessed 17 February 2018) |
| National Archives | History resources for schools and access to expertise and a virtual classroom | www.nationalarchives.gov.uk/education/ (accessed 17 February 2018) |

To view web pages such as those listed in Table 5.2, you need a **web browser**, the most well known of which are Microsoft's **Internet Explorer**, Google's **Chrome**, Apple's **Safari** and The Mozilla Foundation's **Firefox**. VLEs sometimes have compatibility issues with certain browsers; you will need to check with your university's IT department.

The cloud

The 'cloud' has been a buzzword in computing for a number of years. Cloud computing means that the software you use – word processing, statistical analysis etc – sits in the cloud on the internet rather than being on your actual computer or server. It is therefore accessed using an internet connection and a browser. It is a very practical and convenient tool which can help you manage your work. However, it may not be as secure as your university networked drive, so make sure anything important is also saved on the latter.

Social media

Social media includes social networking sites such as **Facebook**, **Twitter**, **Instagram** and **YouTube**. It also includes **blogs** and **wikis**. A blog is a public online diary. Well-known blog sites include **WordPress.com** and Google's **Blogger**. A wiki is an online platform that enables people to work collaboratively on documents. (The most well-known collaborative document is **Wikipedia**.) Sites where you can find software to build wikis include **PB Works**, **PmWiki**, **TWiki** and **MediaWiki**. Social media is quite a contentious area with many concerns over online behaviour and security, some of which will be discussed in the next section.

Online behaviour and security

When using communication software and the internet, it is necessary to demonstrate a degree of caution. There are two big safety threats when you are online: the first is to the actual computer you are using; the second is to yourself.

Computer security

The big threat to computers, especially those connected to the internet, is 'malware', ie malicious software. The most common type of malware is the computer virus, which can destroy data and corrupt your system; other types include 'spyware', software that is designed to steal personal information such as the sites you visit or even your passwords. To protect against threats to the computer you are using, you need to ensure that your computer's operating system is up to date and that you have anti-virus and anti-spyware software installed. Universities often make anti-virus packages such as **Sophos** and **McAfee** freely available to their registered students.

Personal security

The online threat to you personally may be an attempt to steal your identity, or it may be an actual threat to your safety from another person. But the risk can also be to your reputation. Damage to your reputation or image can have far-reaching consequences: poor behaviour, an unguarded comment or an embarrassing photograph could be seen by a prospective employer, for example. The code of good manners and behaviour online is known as **netiquette** (a portmanteau of 'etiquette' – good manners in social interaction – and 'internet'). Netiquette is part of the professional behaviour that is expected of students and those working in caring professions like teaching. The rules of netiquette aim to protect you and others from harm and embarrassment. They require you to behave with politeness and to avoid the following.

- Inappropriate emails. You are in a professional relationship with staff, and the emails you write to them should not contain things you might send to friends, such as slang or kisses.
- 'Empty' emails, with just an attachment but no information. All emails to staff should contain:
  - a clear subject heading, eg 'Group presentation slides';
  - a polite salutation with the correct name, eg 'Dear Dr Gonzalez';
  - a clear, concise message, eg 'Please find attached ...';
  - a polite sign-off, eg 'Regards, Peter'.
- Lack of patience in relation to responses to emails. Academic staff are very busy so don't expect an immediate response; it isn't unreasonable to expect a response within 48 hours, but remember, some staff are part time and may not look at their emails every day.
- Forwarding dubious emails: this includes chain emails or likely hoaxes.
- Posting personal information on discussion boards. This includes information about yourself, other students and your lecturers.
- Adopting an inappropriate tone or language on discussion boards. This includes being careful about upper-case words and exclamation marks, which can seem a bit angry in a discussion context.

CROSS
REFERENCE

*Communication
Skills,*
Chapter 6,
Networking

The university library

The focal point for your university's study resources will be the library. The importance of the university library cannot be overestimated: it is the hub of all scholarly institutions. Academic libraries provide access to specialist textbooks and journals that you will not find in your local library. Moreover, modern academic libraries are now so much more than collections of books housed under the library roof (though this is still an important part of what they do); they are also the source of huge amounts of information and advice which can help you in all aspects of your learning and development. Advances in technology mean that many modern library services are electronic or online, creating a 'virtual library'. You will be able to access many materials and services without actually having to walk into the university library building at all.

Your university library will almost certainly have a specific web page for education students, and may well have a specialist education library. University libraries also provide many other services such as:

- inter-library loans;
- photocopying, scanning and printing services;
- librarians – the most useful resource in the library!

Don't be afraid to ask librarians for help – that is why they are there! They have huge amounts of expertise, often specialising in particular subjects. They are perhaps better regarded as 'information specialists'. Check your library website to see which librarian specialises in education.

Knowing what's out there

Be aware of the different resources available to you in the library and its online virtual counterpart, including the following.

- **Textbooks**: these can be either *standard* textbooks, ie written by one author or a small number of co-authors working together on the text, or *edited* textbooks, ie where different authors (sometimes including the editor/editors) write each chapter separately, and the editor's job is to give the book overall consistency. This distinction is important when it comes to referencing. Many textbooks will be available as ebooks.

- **Academic journals and periodicals**: these are published at regular intervals and reflect advances in a particular area represented by the title itself. Journals are the more academic of the two: they are peer reviewed, ie the articles in them have been subject to a review by an expert panel of referees. With periodicals, it tends to be the editor who decides what is published. In education, important journals include:

  — *Review of Educational Research*;
  — *The Journal of Educational Research*;
  — *Journal of Teacher Education*;
  — *British Journal of Educational Studies*;
  — *British Journal of Special Education*.

CROSS
REFERENCE

Academic Writing and Referencing, Chapter 3, Referring to sources

Periodicals include:

— *Education Today*;

— *Teach Primary Magazine*;

— *English 4–11*.

There is a hierarchy of journals and periodicals: some carry more weight than others. This weight is measured in academia by something called an **impact factor** (Garfield, 2006). As you progress through your academic studies, you will be expected to be more dependent on these weightier journals. Most of these journals and periodicals are available online and you will often have free-of-charge access to them via your university library.

- **Reference material**: this includes dictionaries, encyclopaedias, directories, registers and official reports.

- **Bibliographies, indices and abstracts**: these are special publications which list and summarise all the articles which have been published in a given subject over a specific period of time. For example, the 2015 volume of the BEI (British Education Index) lists all the papers published on education in 2015. It provides information on research, policy and practice in education and training in the UK. It covers all aspects of education from preschool to higher education from sources mostly published in the UK, although it does include international literature. Publication types include:

  — journal articles

  — theses and dissertations

  — conferences and conference papers

  — books

  — reports

- **Official reports and papers**: these could be Acts of Parliament, or reports from government, statuary bodies or voluntary organisations. A lot of these documents are now published only online, usually as a free PDF.

- **Online newspapers**.

Conducting a literature search

If you are writing an essay or giving a presentation, you will probably need to do a substantial amount of academic reading. Firstly, you must know how to find suitable reading material through a systematic search of the literature on that topic. Your literature search should start with the online **library search**. When you type in your search term, say 'phonics', you will usually be given a list of books, articles etc related to the topic. Links will tell you where to locate the book in the library or provide links to ebooks and full-text copies of articles to download to your computer. (You should read the **abstract** of an article to check it really is of use before you print it out: this will save you time and money!). Particularly as you progress in your studies, you will need to consult **databases** such as **BEI** for a more comprehensive search. There will be links to these interfaces, and information about the databases they provide access to, on your university library website. You can also consult your lecturers and the librarians for advice.

Identifying key search terms

Identifying key words related to your assignment will help point you in the right direction. This can involve **lateral thinking**, but this is something you're probably already used to from your own Google searches. For example, if you are looking for a flight from London to New York, you might try some of the following (in combination perhaps) to drive your search:

flights, low-cost flights, Heathrow, Gatwick, JFK, British Airways, Newark, American Airlines, United Airlines

Figure 5.2: Flight search terms

Task

Which key words might you try when researching the following topics?

1) classroom management and challenging behaviour

2) supporting pupils who are on the autism spectrum

Refining your search

A general online library search on a common topic will generally present you with an overwhelming amount of material, so you will need to refine your search. The best way to do this is to use the **advanced search** options provided on the university library website or database interface to limit your search in some way. This could mean refining your search by date or author, for example. A particularly useful advanced search option is to combine one search item with another, eg 'behaviour' and 'ADHD'.

Widening your search

Sometimes your search might not produce many results. In this case, you should try to be more creative with your searches.

- Use synonyms. For example, if the topic is 'children's views on poetry', synonyms for 'child' might be 'young person' or 'adolescent', and 'perceptions', 'experiences' or 'satisfaction' could be substituted for 'views'.

- Use truncation or wildcards. Truncation allows you to search for words with a common stem. The symbol for truncation varies across systems but it is often an asterisk (*). So the search teach* will find 'teach', 'teacher', 'teaching'. A wildcard (again, often an asterisk) can represent any character, so 'wom*n' would find 'woman' and 'women'.

- As you read, make a note of any relevant or interesting references which may enrich your search. (Always make a note of the full reference.)

Top tips

Visit the library!

With all the online tools and materials available, some students find they rarely visit the actual library. However, it can be a great place to study without distractions. Moreover, actually visiting the shelves where you know there are books on your topic, and spending some time browsing the surrounding books can be an interesting way of exploring a topic. Sometimes in this virtual world, it can be nice to feel a book in your hand!

Google and Wikipedia

Google and Wikipedia are useful resources in everyday life but they have serious limitations in academic life. Broadly speaking, the quality of the results generated by Google is not controlled. This contrasts with academic databases like BEI, which only contain *academic* material.

Reflection

Search for 'phonics' and 'spelling' on Google and BEI and compare the results.

There are stronger arguments in favour of using **Google Scholar**, which does have a higher degree of quality control compared to a normal Google search. However, there are still downsides, so you should use it with caution.

- It does not have the sophisticated filters of academic interfaces.
- Companies can pay Google or manipulate searches so that they feature at the top of a Google search.
- You don't often get easy access to the full article: you may be asked to pay or you may need to get to it via an alternative route using the university website, which is more time consuming than if you'd gone there in the first place!

Wikipedia is a general encyclopaedia, and thus, like all encyclopaedias, it is usually not specialised enough for most academic study. Furthermore, it is written by whosoever feels inclined to contribute, which means that the expertise of the writer cannot be guaranteed. Also, there are no peer reviewers to call the writer to account. Finally, Wikipedia is rather strange in that it generates its own references (in hyperlinks throughout the entries), a practice that would be frowned upon in academic circles.

Summary

This chapter has explored how technological and university library resources can support your university studies, particularly in terms of research and communication. It has discussed the potentially positive impact of computer technology and the internet, as well as the challenges they present. Judicious use of technology and the university library, in both its physical and virtual forms, will help you function successfully as a student in the modern world.

Reference

Garfield, E (2006) The History and Meaning of the Journal Impact Factor. *JAMA*, 295(1): 90–3 [online]. Available at: http://garfield.library.upenn.edu/papers/jamajif2006.pdf (accessed 16 February 2018).

Chapter 6
Assessment

Learning outcomes

After reading this chapter you will:

- have gained an overview of assessment in HE;
- be better equipped to approach assessment and deal with stress and anxiety caused by it;
- have gained an understanding of the different types of assessment common in universities and education degrees;
- be aware of the importance of feedback in your academic development;
- be more able to interpret feedback from tutors.

Assessment is an integral part of student life. Different people respond in different ways to assessment, but most people find it challenging. It is very important to be well informed on this aspect of your studies, and to develop strategies to enable you to perform to the very best of your ability in essays, exams, presentations, and practical assessments. You also need to manage the stress and anxiety associated with assessment. This chapter will examine the aims of assessment and explain how it is carried out in HE. It will help you to approach assessment tasks in a positive way, and to understand the crucial role that feedback from your tutors plays in your academic development.

Reflection

1) What kind of assessment have you done in the past?
2) How did you feel about it?
3) Did you feel it was a fair test of your knowledge and abilities?

Assessment in higher education

As a student teacher, you will be assessed through coursework, exams and assessments of your practical teaching ability. These provide **evidence** of your knowledge and understanding of the subject matter of your degree programme, and of your ability to apply it to teaching practice. Assessments in HE have different purposes, depending on the stage you are at in your studies, as illustrated in Table 6.1.

Table 6.1: Assessment types

TYPE OF ASSESSMENT	PURPOSE	IN OTHER WORDS ...
Diagnostic	To determine your current level of knowledge and skills	What do I know?
Formative	To give you a chance to practise something, or to start something and receive feedback before continuing	How am I doing?
Summative	To sum up/establish what you have learned and/or can do and assign a mark/grade based on that performance	How did I do?

CROSS REFERENCE

Chapter 1, Studying education in higher education, Courses and credits

Summative assessment of a module is directly related to the **learning outcomes** of the course module – what you should be able to *understand* or *do*.

If you are an international student, you will normally be required to provide evidence of your English language proficency in order to be accepted onto a university course. This is normally through a particular type of summative test, usually the International English Language Testing System (IELTS) or the Test of English as a Foreign Language (TOEFL).

Submission and marking of assessments

Currently, most universities require students to submit written assessments on their VLE using plagiarism-detection software such as **Turnitin**, which compares your writing with published sources and other submitted essays to ensure it is all your own work. You may also be asked to submit other items, such as presentation slides.

There are many safeguards in place to ensure that the assessment procedure is fair and transparent.

- Submission procedures are usually designed to make all work anonymous.
- A proportion of assignments are moderated (marked by the main assessor and a second marker) for consistency.
- An external examiner (an academic from another university) reviews the assessments, the assessment process and the marks to make sure that everything is fair and consistent.

Most assessed work is marked using **descriptors** which specify the **criteria** that you need to meet in order to achieve a particular mark. These will be closely aligned to the **learning outcomes** of the module and may well be referred to in lectures, seminars etc.

An effective approach to assessment

In order to do well in assessments, it is necessary to approach them in a systematic way.

Inform yourself

It is very important to start an assessment by informing yourself. This means reading the **assessment guidelines** and familiarising yourself with the marking descriptors. It may also involve discussing any queries you have regarding the assessment with your lecturer. This essential familiarisation process is sometimes overlooked: it is not unknown for students to glance at an essay title and go off and write something vaguely connected which they rather fancy writing but which, unfortunately, doesn't address the task! Such an essay may be interesting, and even well written, but if it does not answer the question or address the task, follow the guidelines, or meet the relevant marking criteria, it will not get a high mark. Lecturers do not enjoy giving low marks, but they can only give high marks if the precise criteria in the descriptors are met.

Plan and manage your time

Give yourself a timetable for completing course assignments and stick to it as closely as possible. This timetable should cover:

- familiarising yourself with the assessment guidelines and marking criteria;
- brainstorming your current knowledge of the topic;
- reviewing lecture notes;
- conducting a literature search;
- reading;
- writing an essay/report/presentation plan or outline (which can be revisited and refined);
- writing a first draft of an essay/report or creating draft slides for a presentation;
- editing and redrafting written work or presentation slides;
- formatting your work;
- proofreading your work;
- practising presentations;
- double-checking the assessment guidelines and marking criteria to make sure you have met all the requirements.

An important aspect of assessment is **time management**. You should make sure you start assignments in good time. Begin by reading the guidelines and marking criteria straight away, so that you have time to make an appointment with a lecturer if you need to raise any queries. It is also important to start planning and writing as soon as possible. You may sometimes be able to submit a plan or first draft to your lecturer; be sure to use the feedback from this to help you improve your assignment.

Planning gives you control and a sense of progress, and breaking down a large task into smaller manageable chunks can help you avoid stress and anxiety.

Written assessments

Written assessments test both your understanding of the topic and your academic writing skills. Your assessments may include:

- reports;
- portfolios, which might include written reflections and personal journals or logs;
- essays;
- dissertations.

Reports

Reports require you to present information accurately, usually following a very precise structure. For example, you might be asked to write a report on an individual (anonymised or hypothetical) pupil with headings such as:

- background information;
- strengths in reading;
- aspects of reading which require attention;
- suggested remedial activities;
- review period.

Portfolios

These are a collection of materials which provide evidence of your performance in a number of areas. You might be assessed on the individual items (eg written reflections) and/or the overall coherence of the portfolio. Portfolio assessments often include an assessment on your capacity to demonstrate self-awareness and reflection.

CROSS REFERENCE

Chapter 3, Joining your academic and professional community, Reflective practice

Essays

An essay is a response to a question or statement which requires you to explore a particular topic in detail. This usually involves the development of an argument and the expression of an independent viewpoint, emerging from your engagement with critical debate in the literature. In education, you may be asked to write a reflective essay, in which you analyse your experiences and their impact on your development. Essays vary in form and length, but they usually have the following in common:

- a precise **purpose**, detailed in the essay question or the prescriptions of the essay title;
- a target **reader** – lecturers may ask you to imagine addressing an educated non-expert or a first-year undergraduate (to make sure that you explicitly demonstrate your understanding and do not just expect the reader to read between the lines);

CROSS
REFERENCE

*Academic
Writing and
Referencing*

- a particular **structure**, usually indicated by **headings** and **sub-headings**;

- a formal, objective **academic writing style**;

- **references** to the literature on the topic, presented according to standard referencing conventions: in education, the **Harvard** (name–date) system tends to be used.

Dissertations

CROSS
REFERENCE

Chapter 3,
Becoming
a member
of your
academic and
professional
community,
Advanced
skills,
Research
reports

At the end of your course, you will most likely be required to write a long evidence-based or research-focused essay usually between 10,000 and 20,000 words. This is known as a **dissertation**. For many students, this is the first time they have attempted such an extended piece of work, and it can be quite a daunting prospect. You might be able to find copies of past dissertations in your university library or by asking your lecturers, and looking at these will help you understand what you need to produce.

Like all the work you do at university, a dissertation must be 'original'. This does not mean that you are expected to make a major discovery in your field! It might mean, for example, that you conduct your own review of the evidence related to a particular issue or aspect of teaching and learning such as boys' writing. Undergraduate education students are often required to produce research dissertations, and these may involve empirical studies carried out in schools. Ethical approval may be required before you can undertake such a study.

Oral assessments

CROSS
REFERENCE

*Academic
Writing and
Referencing*

Oral assessments are usually academic presentations, but you may also be assessed on seminar participation in some courses. Rarely for undergraduate students, though almost always used as part of PhD thesis assessments, the *viva voce* (usually shortened to *viva*) is a specific form of oral assessment.

Presentations test your understanding of the topic, your oral communication skills and your use of presentation software such as PowerPoint or Prezi. You may be asked to do individual or group presentations. Some presentations may be 'poster' presentations, where you talk around a poster containing an overview of your topic – these can also be done by individuals or groups. Group presentations partly test your collaborative skills; poster presentations will particularly test your ability to convey information and ideas in a concise, visually appealing form.

Top tips

Public speaking: reducing stress and anxiety

Most people suffer nerves when speaking in public – the proverbial 'butterflies' in the stomach! It is actually a good sign in a way – it shows you care about what you are doing and have respect for your audience. However, there are some strategies that you can adopt to help stem the nerves a little and reduce stress and anxiety.

1) **Keep it simple**. Complex content benefits from a **simple organisational structure**, and the simpler it is, the easier it is to remember.

2) **Use an *aide-memoire***. This is usually in the form of brief notes on cards. Some people find it useful to note down 'transition' phrases such as 'I'll now move on to discuss some of the limitations of the study' to help them move between slides (often the point when you lose your train of thought). Presentation software often allows notes to be made that the presenter can see but not the audience.

3) **Practise**. Practise several times to help you remember what you want to say, improve your delivery and increase your confidence.

4) **Check the pronunciation of key words**. Use an online dictionary with sound function (or a specialised reference work for very technical words), especially if English is not your first language. Assessors will not penalise you for having an accent (we all do!) or for the occasional mispronunciation, but they will be irritated if you keep mispronouncing a key word, or they will be unable to follow if they cannot make out which word you are trying to say. Being prepared will reduce anxiety.

CROSS REFERENCE

Chapter 5, Academic resources: technology and the library, Presentations

5) **Don't learn by rote**. Practice does not mean learning by rote – each practice attempt should follow the same basic structure, perhaps with some repeated phrases written down as an aide-memoire, but there should also be some normal variation. It will sound unnatural if you try to recite something you have memorised, and straining to remember will make you stressed and preoccupied, preventing engagement with the audience.

CROSS REFERENCE

Communication Skills, Chapter 1, Academic presentations and public speaking

6) **Don't panic**. If you lose your train of thought, pause and consult your notes or slides. Audiences are usually fairly sympathetic – they probably know how you feel!

7) **Slow down**. It's quite common for people to speak too quickly in presentations, especially if they are nervous. Make a conscious effort to slow down, pause occasionally and breathe! You will then feel more in control.

Exams

Exams are a way of checking that you understand the core work covered on a course. Exams have many different forms and functions, but they all test your ability to recall information under strict time constraints, a very useful skill in education practice.

Exams can be 'seen', whereby you are given the topic beforehand and can prepare your answer, or 'unseen', whereby you can be asked to answer questions about anything you have studied on a particular module. Some exams are 'open-book', which means you can consult books, articles and materials during the exam. Some exams are multiple choice, requiring you to select the right answer from the given options. Alternatively, you may be required to provide short or long written answers to questions. Examples of education exam questions are given below.

Example exam questions

Multiple choice

Which of these words is not a compound word?

   a) football

   b) hairbrush

   c) dislike

   d) headteacher

Which of the words below does not contain a digraph?

   a) sock

   b) weak

   c) shed

   d) blast

Short answer

Describe a spelling rule or spelling generalisation for making words which end with y into plurals. The singulars and plurals below should help you:

lady – ladies

pony – ponies

key – keys

toy – toys

donkey – donkeys

Long answer

1) Myhill et al (2011) examined ways of developing children's writing and discovered that 'actively engaging children with grammar through writing was more effective than teaching grammar as a separate topic'. Discuss with reference to your background reading and your experience in schools.

2) With reference to your background reading, justify the importance of reading for pleasure in a primary classroom.

Top tips

Past papers

Universities provide online access to past exam papers, usually through their library websites. Looking at these as part of your revision can be an invaluable aid in helping you to understand the types of questions you may be asked.

Testing your recall against these can also make you aware of gaps in your knowledge which you need to revise.

Exam technique

There are certain strategies that you can adopt during an exam which will help you perform to the best of your ability and help you manage stress and anxiety.

1) **Check the whole paper**. Read it through at the beginning and make sure you are clear about how many questions you need to answer and how many marks will be awarded for each question.

2) **Manage your time**. Allot a certain amount of time to each question or section and stick to it. When the time is up, move on to the next part even if you haven't finished – you have more of a chance of a high mark if you provide unfinished answers for four out of four questions; two out of four questions, no matter how well answered, may well only give you a mark out of a maximum of 50%.

3) **Answer the question**. Read and highlight key terms, and quickly plan an answer which addresses the question. Then stick to it.

4) **Make your writing legible**. You cannot be given credit for something if the marker cannot read it.

Practical teaching assessments

Education degrees which include the award of qualified teacher status (QTS) require students' practical teaching to be assessed against the Teachers' Standards. These state:

> The Teachers' Standards are used to assess all trainees working towards QTS, and all those completing their statutory induction period. They are also used to assess the performance of all teachers with QTS who are subject to The Education (School Teachers' Appraisal) (England) Regulations 2012, and may additionally be used to assess the performance of teachers who are subject to these regulations and who hold qualified teacher learning and skills (QTLS) status.

When you are going to be observed (and at all other times), you should ensure you provide clear lesson plans so that observers can see what your intended learning outcomes are and how you intend to achieve them. You will also need to show the resources you will use and how you will organise your lesson, as well as where the lesson features in a sequence of lessons.

Remember that observers' feedback is intended to help you to develop as a teacher and that you should use it to help you to reflect on and improve your practice. Nowadays, experienced teachers are used to being observed by their peers and the best professionals welcome constructive criticism, as well as praise, and see it as important to their professional development.

Feedback on academic work

One of the most important roles that lecturers perform is to give feedback to students on the work they produce. There are two types of feedback: **formative** and **summative** (see Table 6.1). Formative feedback is advice on how you can improve your work in a current or future task. It can be given for both assessed and non-assessed assignments. Summative feedback is the feedback you receive on an assessed piece of work, often at the end of a module or programme of study, to enable you to understand why a particular mark has been awarded; it tells you how you have met, or failed to meet, the marking criteria attached to the task. It may be combined with formative feedback if appropriate.

These days, feedback on written assignments is often provided on VLEs. Students can access their assignment and view comments posted in the text itself, and in the accompanying critical commentary.

No matter what mark you receive for an assignment, it is very important to know why you did or didn't do well. It is crucial that you access and understand feedback, whether it be provided on your VLE or in conversation with a lecturer. Your response to feedback will help determine your future academic development.

Universities are becoming increasingly aware of the importance of good feedback to students. This has been underlined by the introduction of the National Student Survey (see www.thestudentsurvey.com), a survey of all final-year undergraduates in the UK to assess their opinions of the quality of their degree programmes. You should be aware of what systems your university has in place to enable it to meet the requirements of students. You should also be aware of what constitutes good practice in terms of providing feedback.

Good practice in feedback

Feedback should be:

1) **Transparent**. It should be clear how the mark was arrived at. This may involve highlighting of the descriptors or comments which directly refer to these.

2) **Constructive**. The marker should provide clear, helpful suggestions on how you can improve.

3) **Personalised**. The feedback should be clearly related to your unique piece of work. It should also be geared towards your own personal academic development.

4) **Timely**. Feedback dates should be given in advance. These dates should be made in time to inform any future assignments.

5) **Ongoing**. Feedback is not confined to assessments; you should receive feedback regularly, in class, in teaching practice, and through the VLE.

Your response to feedback

It is important that you do not waste the valuable resource that feedback is. You should always:

1) **Be proactive**. Seek out feedback by reading all your university emails and checking your VLE on a regular basis. If you don't understand the feedback, email your lecturer to make an appointment, or visit them during office hours.

2) **Be reflective**. Read or listen to feedback very carefully and make sure it makes sense to you. Consider feedback with reference to the assessment guidelines and descriptors – did you understand the task and follow instructions? Be honest with yourself about whether or not the mark and the feedback match your own expectations and the effort you put in. What can you learn from the comments? What insights can you gain on your strengths and weaknesses? Is there anything you need to do differently in future assignments?

3) **Be realistic**. If there seems to be rather a lot of negative feedback, it is easy to feel overwhelmed. Try to pull out three things which seem to be particularly important (common areas of concern include: lack of a clear structure; overly descriptive work, lacking in critical analysis; lack of research or understanding; poor grammar/punctuation/sentence structure), or which have also been mentioned in other feedback.

How you respond to feedback will partly determine your academic and professional development. It is hard to hear criticism, but it is crucial not to take it personally: the feedback is about your assignment; it is not about you. The main objective of feedback is to help you, so you need to approach it with this in mind. Before you look at feedback, prepare yourself mentally to look for things to learn rather than things to dwell on negatively. It is largely how you react to constructive criticism which will determine how you develop in your study and work life.

Case studies

Look at the marks and feedback received by student teachers for their essays, and answer the questions below.

1) What can each student learn from the comments?
2) What are the strengths and weaknesses of the essay?
3) What action should the student take immediately or in the long term?
4) What should the student do differently in the next assignment?
5) What three points should the student focus on?

Student 1

Overall mark awarded: 58%

- Interpretation of source material 54%

    You have conveyed a reasonable understanding of the material presented, though there is some irrelevant or peripheral material in your submission.

- Critical ability 58%

  You have made some good critical comments about some of the source material you have looked at but, in some of the material, you missed some of the major shortcomings.

- Research awareness 52%

  You have a reasonable understanding of the research methodologies employed in the source material you used, though there were some misunderstandings and inaccuracies in your interpretation.

- Style and presentation 76%

  A well-written piece, with a logical flow and a high standard of English; presented to a high standard.

- Referencing and use of the literature 55%

  Reasonable range of scholarly reviews and sources consulted; some referencing errors both in-text and in the construction of the final reference list.

- Application to practice 52%

  A reasonable attempt to link theory to practice, though some of the links you made were a little weak.

Student 2

Overall mark awarded: 82%

- Interpretation of source material 84%

  You have thoroughly rejected inappropriate and irrelevant source material and have accurately and confidently conveyed understanding of the material you have used.

- Critical ability 78%

  You fully understand the source material you have used, making detailed and appropriate critical comments; strong arguments have been made throughout the submission, occasionally you have missed a key shortcoming in one of the sources consulted.

- Research awareness 82%

  You have a thorough understanding of the research methodologies employed in the source material you consulted, accurately describing, interpreting and evaluating those methodologies. You were very slightly confused over some statistical elements but these are complex areas that many graduates, get confused about.

- Style and presentation 88%

  Extremely well-written piece, with a logical flow; presented to a very high standard with few typographical, grammatical or spelling errors.

- Referencing and use of the literature 75%

  Extensive range of scholarly reviews and sources consulted; there were a few minor referencing errors.

↑• Application to practice 82%

Clear links between the material you cited and teaching practice; clear evidence of evidence-based practice; some additional practice examples would have enhanced the submission.

Summary

This chapter has examined the aims of assessment and detailed the assessment procedure in higher education. It has provided advice on how to approach assessment tasks, manage stress and anxiety, and achieve success. Finally, it has discussed the issue of feedback and the crucial role it plays in your academic development.

Reference

Myhill, D, Lines, H & Watson, A (2011) *Making Meaning with Grammar: a repertoire of possibilities*. University of Exeter.

Appendix:
The language of higher education

Assessment	Tasks and processes used to determine the level of your knowledge and skills
Blended learning	Learning which combines traditional classroom study and web-based learning
Collaborative learning	Working collectively and co-operatively with other students
Continuing professional development (CPD)	The learning activities that professionals engage in, in order to develop their knowledge and skills throughout their career
Credit	Credits are awarded to students in recognition of the completion of a unit. (The number of credits allocated is based on the notional hours of learning needed to complete the unit successfully.)
Critical thinking	The process of analysing and evaluating information and ideas, and demonstrating how this process has informed your own understanding, ideas and opinions
Degree	A qualification awarded on successful completion of a course in HE
Diploma	A qualification awarded by a university, which is at a lower level than a degree
Directed study	Independent study under the guidance of a staff member
Distance learning	Learning where the student mainly studies from home via correspondence, using web-based resources – perhaps occasionally attending university workshops etc
Facilitator	A teacher who helps facilitate your learning rather than teaching you directly, enabling a two-way process between student and teacher
Formative	Describes work that you are asked to do which is developmental rather than formally assessed (compare with summative)
Further education (FE)	Education beyond secondary school but at pre-degree level
Higher education (HE)	Education at university level, including certificates, diplomas and degrees
Independent learning	Learning which is directed by the student

Learning outcomes	What you will be able to do or understand by the end of the course
Lecture	An educational talk to a (usually large) group of students
Lecturer	A member of staff who has significant teaching, and often significant research, commitments
Lifelong learning	Refers to a view that learning occurs throughout life and that there are opportunities for learning at all ages and not just when you are a child or young adult (a view that is supported by the government and most educators)
Module	One of the units that make up a complete course at university
Office hours	The times when your lecturer is officially available, usually to discuss problems or queries, or to provide individual guidance
Portfolio	A personal record (normally written) of your learning experiences (increasingly seen as a valuable tool to aid student learning; the best portfolios include reflective aspects)
Postgraduate	Study undertaken once you have a Bachelor's degree (two further degrees are available at postgraduate level – the Master's degree and the Doctorate – though sub-degree awards such as Postgraduate Certificates (PGCert) and Postgraduate Diploma (PGDip) may also be available).
Problem-based learning (PBL)	PBL is a form of 'enquiry-based learning' (EBL), an umbrella term for learning in groups where enquiry (asking questions and investigating) is central to the process. It is an innovative type of learning designed to help students develop their thought processes (and, indeed, their teaching practice). PBL involves finding solutions to real-world problems by working co-operatively with other students. In PBL, teachers act as facilitators rather than teachers.
Professor	A senior grade of the teaching/research staff, normally given for exceptional contribution to a particular field of study
Programme of study	The overall course of study you are undertaking, such as a diploma or degree
Reflection	Thinking about and questioning your own experiences, thoughts and behaviour in order to enhance personal, academic and professional development
Seminar	A formally timetabled, small group discussion normally facilitated by a teacher or lecturer
Student autonomy	The ability to take charge of your own learning and development

Summative	Describes work that you are asked to do which is formally assessed, and must be completed and passed if you are to continue your programme of study (compare with formative)
Syllabus	A description of the content you will cover in the module or course
Tertiary education	Education beyond secondary school, including further and higher education
Tutorial	Tuition given to an individual or small group
Undergraduate	Study undertaken at or below Bachelor's degree level. The Bachelor's-with-Honours degree is the benchmark university award and in the strictest sense of the word, you don't graduate until you have this degree. Bachelor's degrees are sometimes called 'first degrees' to differentiate them from higher degrees that are normally taken as second or third degrees. Don't confuse these with the gradings (1st, 2:1, 2:2 and 3rd) that are given to first degrees
Virtual Learning Environment (VLE)	A web-based platform to support course delivery in universities
Vocational qualification	Qualification aimed at developing skills for employment, often including work-based experience

Answer key

Chapter 1
Top tips, Lectures (page 9)

4)

eg = for example

NB = note

cf = compare and contrast

ie = that is to say

Chapter 3
Academic phrasebank, Task (pages 37–38)

A5, B4, C3, D1, E7, F6

Chapter 4
Scrutinising research and arguments, Task (page 57)

Premise	Ideas on which subsequent ideas or actions are based
Assumption	Something which is accepted as true without question or proof
Agenda	A reason for doing something which is often not directly declared
Anecdotal	Based on personal experience rather than research
Bias	The action of supporting or opposing someone or something in an unfair way, allowing personal opinion to influence your judgement
Subjective	Based on personal beliefs and feelings, rather than on facts
Unsubstantiated	Not supported by facts

Scrutinising research and arguments, Task (pages 59–61)

Why do we need research?

Imagine going to see your local doctor and hearing her (or him) say, 'Oh I don't keep up to date with research. I just use the things that I know work for my patients. I learned what I know on the job, so I'm not really interested in how research can help me or my patients'. Would you be impressed? Of course, medical research and educational research are different, but we can still learn valuable lessons from what research tells us will help make us more effective teachers, which will keep us up to date with evidence as it develops, and which will help keep us effective and fresh as teachers through trying out and evaluating new ideas.

General context for chapter

In this chapter, you will find evidence from research which will help you reflect critically on the teaching of literacy in schools, by comparing what we do with other countries and by looking at some examples of research evidence about what has helped in the teaching of literacy.

International comparisons

There are a number of large-scale international comparisons of educational performance. The oldest is the Trends in International Mathematics and Science Study (TIMSS), which was first administered in 1995 by the International Association for the Evaluation of Educational Achievement (IEA) to allow the countries involved to compare their pupils' educational attainment in mathematics and science. The IEA also manages the Progress in International Reading Literacy Study (PIRLS), which assesses 9-10-year-olds in reading and literacy (see below). The Programme for International Student Assessment (PISA) is another international study, undertaken by the Organisation for Economic Co-operation and Development (OECD), of 15-year-old school pupils' attainment in mathematics, science, and reading. It was first administered in 2000 and then repeated every three years. These studies can help us to understand how our children are learning compared with progress other countries. They also can shed light on other debates, such as the age that children start school, and on the teaching of the subjects that are assessed, including literacy. The tests and the design of the sampling of pupils aim to make the fairest comparisons possible, given differences in language and culture.

General context: provides international context

Progress in International Reading Literacy Study (PIRLS) 2011

The Progress in International Reading Literacy Study (PIRLS) is an international study of reading. It is conducted by the International Association for the Evaluation of Educational Achievement (IEA). It has measured trends in the reading and literacy achievement of 9-10 year-olds every five years since 2001. It also collects information about reading and literacy policies, teaching practices in schools and home experiences. In 2006 PIRLS tested over 215,000 pupils aged 9-10 years, from 45 countries.

In 2011, the results showed that only five out of the 45 countries involved performed significantly better than England. These countries were Hong Kong, the Russian Federation, Singapore, Finland and Northern Ireland.

Reference to key research

England's performance improved between 2006 and 2011. Only the United States and Chinese Taipei showed greater improvement in this period.

Pupils in England had a wider spread of attainment than the top performing countries. The highest attaining pupils in England were similar to those in Singapore and higher than the best readers in the three top performing countries (Hong Kong, the Russian Federation and Finland). However, low attaining pupils in England scored less well than the low attaining pupils in other countries.

This indicates that overall progress in reading at primary school in England and Northern Ireland is good compared with other countries around the world (Scotland did not take part in PIRLS). It also suggests that although the highest attaining pupils in England do as well as the best countries in the world for reading, we are not as good as these countries in supporting the reading achievement of our lower attaining pupils. England had one of the largest proportions of pupils reaching the Advanced International Benchmark (18 per cent). However, the proportion of pupils in England who did not reach the Low International Benchmark (5 per cent) is similar to the proportion that do not achieve level 3 or above in National Curriculum tests of reading in England at the end of primary school. Overall this international evidence therefore suggests that this is an area where we could improve our overall performance, and at the same time provide a more equitable education system for our children. In other countries gap between the highest and lowest attaining pupils does not widen as much as it does in England.

Summary to clarify interpretation of research findings

Gender and attainment in literacy

International comparisons can provide information about
more than overall national performance or the spread
of scores however. We worry a lot in the UK about the
underperformance of boys and the difficulties that boys seem
to have in literacy and in particular early reading and writing,
but what is the evidence for this from PIRLS? It is certainly true
that girls performed significantly better than boys in PIRLS
in England, but this is true for almost all other participating
countries and girls scores on average are about 3 per cent better
than boys. So girls all over the world, on average, do a little
bit better on tests of literacy at age 10. It is also true that the
difference between the attainment of boys and girls is a little bit
bigger in England than in most other countries. and this has
stayed about the same all three PIRLS surveys. So the problem
is an international one, and we do a little less well than other
countries at solving it. The difference between the UK and
the average of the other countries is just less than 1 per cent
however. So although there is a difference, and that difference
hasn't really changed since 2001, it is a very small difference.
It is also true to say that the difference between boys and girls
is not as great as the 'gap' between low attaining and high
attaining pupils' results in PIRLS. We have 5 per cent of our
pupils who don't even reach the low benchmark, whereas 99 per
cent of the pupils in Hong Kong, and 98 per cent of the pupils
in the Russian Federation, Sweden and the United States do.

Presentation and interpretation of findings

Discussion versus description, Task (pages 59–60)

Why do we need research?

Imagine going to see your local doctor and hearing her (or
him) say, 'Oh I don't keep up to date with research. I just use
the things that I know work for my patients. I learned what I
know on the job, so I'm not really interested in how research
can help me or my patients'. Would you be impressed?
Of course, medical research and educational research are
different, but we can still learn valuable lessons from what
research tells us will help make us more effective teachers,
which will keep us up to date with evidence as it develops,
and which will help keep us effective and fresh as teachers
through trying out and evaluating new ideas.

Discussion

In this chapter, you will find evidence from research which
will help you reflect critically on the teaching of literacy in
schools, by comparing what we do with other countries and
by looking at some examples of research evidence about what
has helped in the teaching of literacy.

International comparisons

There are a number of large-scale international comparisons of educational performance. The oldest is the Trends in International Mathematics and Science Study (TIMSS), which was first administered in 1995 by the International Association for the Evaluation of Educational Achievement (IEA) to allow the countries involved to compare their pupils' educational attainment in mathematics and science. The IEA also manages the Progress in International Reading Literacy Study (PIRLS), which assesses 9-10-year-olds in reading and literacy (see below). The Programme for International Student Assessment (PISA) is another international study, undertaken by the Organisation for Economic Co-operation and Development (OECD), of 15-year-old school pupils' attainment in mathematics, science, and reading. It was first administered in 2000 and then repeated every three years. These studies can help us to understand how our children are learning compared with progress other countries. They also can shed light on other debates, such as the age that children start school, and on the teaching of the subjects that are assessed, including literacy. The tests and the design of the sampling of pupils aim to make the fairest comparisons possible, given differences in language and culture.

Description

Progress in International Reading Literacy Study (PIRLS) 2011

The Progress in International Reading Literacy Study (PIRLS) is an international study of reading. It is conducted by the International Association for the Evaluation of Educational Achievement (IEA). It has measured trends in the reading and literacy achievement of 9-10 year-olds every five years since 2001. It also collects information about reading and literacy policies, teaching practices in schools and home experiences. In 2006 PIRLS tested over 215,000 pupils aged 9-10 years, from 45 countries.

In 2011, the results showed that only five out of the 45 countries involved performed significantly better than England. These countries were Hong Kong, the Russian Federation, Singapore, Finland and Northern Ireland.

England's performance improved between 2006 and 2011. Only the United States and Chinese Taipei showed greater improvement in this period.

Description

Pupils in England had a wider spread of attainment than the top performing countries. The highest attaining pupils in England were similar to those in Singapore and higher than the best readers in the three top performing countries (Hong Kong, the Russian Federation and Finland). However, low attaining pupils in England scored less well than the low attaining pupils in other countries.

This indicates that overall progress in reading at primary school in England and Northern Ireland is good compared with other countries around the world (Scotland did not take part in PIRLS). It also suggests that although the highest attaining pupils in England do as well as the best countries in the world for reading, we are not as good as these countries in supporting the reading achievement of our lower attaining pupils. England had one of the largest proportions of pupils reaching the Advanced International Benchmark (18 per cent). However, the proportion of pupils in England who did not reach the Low International Benchmark (5 per cent) is similar to the proportion that do not achieve level 3 or above in National Curriculum tests of reading in England at the end of primary school. Overall this international evidence therefore suggests that this is an area where we could improve our overall performance, and at the same time provide a more equitable education system for our children. In other countries the gap between the highest and lowest attaining pupils does not widen as much as it does in England

Discussion

Chapter 5
Identifying key search terms, Task (Page 79)

1) class management; behaviour; discipline
2) autism; autistic; special needs

Index

Note: *italicised* page numbers are illustrations, **bold** page numbers are tables, and the suffix 'a' refers to the Appendix at the back of the book.